The New Plantation
Lessons from Rikers Island

Jason Trask

DEERBROOK EDITIONS

PUBLISHED BY
Deerbrook Editions
P.O. Box 542
Cumberland, ME 04021
www.issuu.com/deerbrookeditions

FIRST EDITION

ISBN: 978-0-9600293-0-3

Book and cover design by Jeffrey Haste

Author photograph by Eliza Beghe

Contents

In Memory of Stephen E. Ray, a history teacher for whom teaching was primarily about building relationships with students, and secondly, about encouraging them to view the world through their own eyes rather than through the eyes of others.

Acknowledgements

Thank you to Adam Berlin, Dennis Camire, James Cocoros, Kevin Daley, David Daniel, Cris Delcuore, Amy Farranto, Jeffrey Haste, Jeffrey Heiman, Byron Hoot, Kahlil Koromantee, Robert Clyde Lazowsky, Dianne O'Donnell, Emanuel Pariser, David Plick, Diane Simmons, James Wells, Peter Wortsman, and the Tamarack Writers' Group at Big Moose Lake. In one way or another, all of you have helped to make this a better book.

Special thanks to my brother Tim Trask for reading and commenting on the manuscript at various stages of its completion.

Very Special Thanks to my wife Eliza for her love, comments, and support.

Early versions of three of these chapters have appeared elsewhere:

J Journal published "The New Plantation" and "Mountain Man";
Down & Out | The People's Online Magazine published "Why We Should Kill the White Man."

Thank you to both publications.

Author's Note

I have presented my experiences as a teacher on Rikers Island as accurately and realistically as I can. That said, I have taken certain liberties: I changed nearly every individual's name. In some cases, I played with the sequence of events and I combined events into one class that occurred during several classes. From notes, I recreated long and involved conversations that I placed in quotation marks.

I did not, however, take liberties in my presentation of the language I encountered out there. Cursing, swearing, profanity of every conceivable stripe—including racial epithets—constitute the *lingua franca* of prisons and jails. Rikers Island is no exception.

I have changed the spelling of the n-word to a form that some African Americans find more acceptable. I included the word because I saw no other way to recreate the atmosphere of the classrooms in which I taught out there. I apologize to anyone who may be offended by this.

Because the words "Hispanic" and "Asian" are capitalized, I have capitalized the words "Black" and "White" when those words refer to people.

Preface

For three years I taught English to young men on Rikers Island in a school run by the New York City Department of Education in a jail run by the New York City Department of Correction. The marriage between those two agencies did not work out. By the time I arrived on the island, it was as if a divorce had taken place and, through a pre-nup agreement, the DOC was awarded custody of the classrooms and the students. The DOE was awarded nothing but the books, paper, and pencils. While this arrangement made teaching difficult, it was the least of our students' worries.

Most of them were brilliant. This makes sense when you consider that many of them reared themselves in the manner of Huckleberry Finn.

Like Huck, they lived by their wits and spoke from their souls. Their honesty was stunning. Which is not to say they never lied and never stole. On the other hand, we all know people who never lie and never steal, yet are full of deceit. Certainly Huck did his share of lying and stealing, but—as was true of my students—it would be difficult to find someone as honest.

Now, I don't mean that I would hold them up as models for all of humanity. Among other things, many of them had a history of violence. But that doesn't mean they lacked conscience, which seems to be the assumption behind a good deal of the so-called professional literature on the subject of incarcerated juveniles. They may have done things most of us would never do. But look at the world from their perspective and their choices make a kind of moral sense.

The way they see it, they have been kept from getting the things most other people take for granted—the things I take for granted. Not only material possessions, but such luxuries as an education and a future. They see themselves as living under the occupation of a hostile army, a.k.a., the police. For them, this is an army that kills kids who look like they do.

To varying degrees, we all know they have a point. I certainly knew it even before stepping foot onto Rikers. The thing is, I knew it only with my head. Rikers hammered that knowledge into my heart. And, sure, I was aware that White Privilege exists. I just wasn't aware of the degree to which it exists for me.

By the time I left the island, there was no way to deny any of this, nor to deny that America's reliance on incarceration is racist. Of the 200 plus students who came through my classroom, only five were non-Hispanic Whites. What's worse is my experience fit the trend.

In America today, one Black man in three will be incarcerated at some point during his life. One Hispanic man in six will be incarcerated. Yet only one White man in seventeen will have that experience.[1]

My students on Rikers grew up knowing instinctively the reality behind those statistics: inequality was to be their lot. How is it in their interest to become model citizens when their dreams have been deferred for four centuries?

I set out to write a memoir about my experiences as a teacher in an alternative setting. Quickly I realized how impossible that would be without addressing the prevalence of racism in our so-called system of justice.

Our best hope is that the system is broken. If it's not, what we have is intentional.

The New Plantation

Lessons from Rikers Island

1. Survival of the Fittest

Mr. Beedy and I were in his classroom when the kids piled in.

"Brooklyn in the house," said one kid as he beat his chest.

"Uptown, representing," said another.

Beedy was a social studies teacher. He told me he liked to work with videos as much as possible. "These kids love to watch videos," he said.

After about twenty kids were in the room, another African American teacher by the name of Mr. Rafter came in and spoke to Mr. Beedy. After he left, Beedy told the kids to make room because Mr. Rafter was bringing his class in as well. Most of the kids moved their chairs back, but a couple ran over to the window to see which room the other kids were from.

"Shit, that's them herb ass niggas from two rooms down."

"Bullshit. Them stank ass mo-fo's ain't coming in here."

"Yo, Mr. Beedy. Don't be lettin' them crack babies up in here, word up."

Now everyone was jostling for a place at the window and they were universally complaining about the kids who were just starting to arrive. But they were also laughing in a friendly way. Mr. Rafter opened the door for them.

"Yo, man. What'cha stink ass niggas comin' in here for?" one of them said to the kids as they entered.

"Stop frontin' and get out the mother fuckin' way. Queens in the house. Representin'."

Another kid said, "Don't you mean…" and in a high falsetto he added, "Queens?"

They came in, some with their chests expanded, others looking wary. They were carrying their own chairs and they jockeyed for the choicest spots. There was a good deal of hostile language and friendly laughter. They settled down and Beedy told them the video they were about to see was about lions and hyenas. Without further ado he pressed "Play."

The kids watched eagerly as the narrator explained where the camera crew had traveled to get these shots and told a little about how difficult it was to survive out there.

"Yo," said one of the students. "That sound like Red Hook to me."

They all laughed, including Beedy who said, "They don't play in Red Hook, right, Seth?"

"Damn straight."

"Shit. Come to Bed-Stuy, you want to learn survival," said another.

"Bed-Stuy ain't shit. Bed-Stuy niggas always be gettin' deaded for they shit, word up. And if they..."

"Men," said Beedy, "you got to keep it down. You all bad—we know that."

The kids laughed and returned to the video.

Laughing hyenas were circling a family of lions. While the adult lions were fending them off, one of the female hyenas was able to sneak in and grab one of the lion cubs and drag it off and kill it.

Immediately, the students were on their feet and screaming with laughter.

"Yo, that nigga don't CARE."

"He from my block, word up."

"That nigga is NIIICE."

"He got them LOVEly moves."

"Yeah, and that little lion nigga, he a herb."

"Word to mother, he a herb."

I realized that I would have never been able to picture such a scenario. It was beyond me. I wondered how much of it was for show.

When a huge adult male lion made his appearance, the room grew quiet.

"Looks to me like HE's the man," said Beedy.

Only a few kids registered the remark. The others watched in silence as he chased down the hyena who had led the attacks on the lions. With one swift cuff of his paw, he tripped the hyena, bit her, and broke her neck.

As the hyena, who moments before had been their hero, lay dying, every kid in the room was on his feet, animated and screaming to each other about how bad that lion was.

"He an uptown nigga," one of them said.

I spotted Beedy watching me and laughing at my reaction as I looked around the room at the kids. I was in a world completely new to me, a world of completely inverted values.

They screamed for Beedy to replay that scene. When he complied, the place erupted into total chaos. Everyone was screaming about how bad that lion was and what a herb that hyena had been.

The video was ending when a kid looked at me and whispered, "Yo, Mr. What you gonna do for them Tims?"

He laughed when I asked him, "What?"

"What you gonna do for them Tims?"

I looked down and realized he meant my Timberland boots.

The kid tapped his friend's shoulder and said, "Yo, let's dead him for his boots."

The other kid looked around, looked at where Beedy and Rafter were sitting as though he was giving it serious consideration. I knew there was no way it was going to happen, but it gave me a small inkling of what this job could be like.

I caught myself at this point and said, "Yo, I'm already wearing them. What '*chu* gonna do for 'em?"

They both laughed and I felt I'd passed their first gate. They asked my name.

"Jason."

"Jason? That your last name?"

"No. My first name. My last name's Trask. What are your names?"

They didn't answer. Instead one of them said, "You be climbin' mountains and shit, right?"

"Yeah, I like to climb mountains."

"I can tell that shit right off."

I was a little stunned. "How could you tell that?"

"Ya'll White people is easy to read. So what you be teachin'?"

"English."

"Where you be teaching at out in the world?"

"Well, the last place I taught was NJIT."

"What's that?"

"New Jersey Institute of Technology."

"High school?"

"No, it's a college."

"You teach college?"

"I did, yeah. Now I'm going to teach here."

"For real? Why you be teachin' here if you was teachin' college?"

"It's more interesting."

"Shit…"

The other kid said, "You ain't no REAL teacher."

They had dismissed me. I didn't know what to say.

Later I met a teacher named Beelman and told him about it. He said they'd dismissed me because I'd given an explanation that didn't involve money or power. "Money and power—those are the only reasons anyone does anything in their world. They're the ultimate materialists. Everything has a material cause. It's a different world."

When I thought about it, I realized I hadn't been completely honest with the kids. I'd taken this job only after being told at a faculty meeting that adjuncts at NJIT weren't being rehired for the coming semester. I wondered if maybe the kids were right.

*   *   *

When I got home that afternoon, there was a message on the phone from the Humanities Chair at NJIT. I returned his call to find he was offering me four courses for the spring semester.

I said, "But I thought you weren't rehiring adjuncts."

"Not all adjuncts," he said.

I had actually enjoyed teaching English out there. Blowing engineering students' minds was a blast—I'd have them read Kafka's "The Metamorphosis" and Melville's "Bartleby the Scribner" and they'd be like, "What was that?"

But the fact was, Rikers had something NJIT would never have, and that was adventure. Not only that, for the first time in my life the adventure route was the more practical one. I actually had a job, a real job, not just a temporary one. Not only would my family and I now have great health insurance: for the first time we'd have dental.

I told him I'd just gotten a full-time job. After asking for details, he had a good laugh and told me if it didn't work out to give him a call.

2. The New Plantation

Earlier that morning, my first, I had been stopped by the Correction Officers just before the bridge that leads to the 413-acre, liver-shaped island in the middle of the East River between Queens and the Bronx.

I was struck by how bored the COs acted. It was as if they were telling me there was nothing I could possibly do that would surprise them. In my younger days, I would have taken that as a challenge—if nothing else, I would have provided them with a bit of Dadaist theater to get them to react. But not today. For the first time in my life I had a chance at a job I actually wanted.

They checked my new ID card and gave me a temporary parking pass. I drove over the three-quarter mile bridge from Queens to the island which was once the primary garbage dump for the City of New York and since the 1930s has been its primary detention center, one of the two or three largest in the world.

Few shopping malls exist with parking lots as huge as those on Rikers Island. For employees only. Visitors park across the bridge.

So, yes, incarceration means jobs, over 10,000 on Rikers alone.

I circled two such parking lots for ten minutes before finding an empty spot by a chain link fence that towered above me. Concertina wire lined its top, a trailing vine of sorts, a metal stand-in for vegetation. But for the barbed razors running along its coiled edges, it resembled a giant Slinky—not one you'd want to meet coming downstairs.

Looking around at the barren landscape, my soul seemed a liability. I sucked it deep within myself and followed other pedestrians across the parking lot to a sidewalk where a CO allowed everyone to pass but me.

I handed him my ID card.

Except for a customs agent in East Berlin, and occasionally my wife, no one has ever observed my face with such attention. That afternoon as I was leaving, he waved me past. For the remainder of that school year and the two that followed, he would never check my ID again. Thousands of people passed this man each day. If you were new, he checked your ID; otherwise, he waved you past.

Inside the Adolescent Reception and Detention Center (ARDC),[2] we passed through a metal detector. By watching the others, I knew to slip my ID through the slot in the window. The CO who took it, plucked a numbered visitor's pass from a giant bulletin board and hung my ID in its place. He handed the pass to me. I clipped it to my shirt as though I knew the routine. By now I was feeling confident. It surprised me when he yelled through the slot, "First time here?"

"Yes."

"Wait."

From my ID he knew where I was going. He got on the phone and told me someone would be right down.

Soon a young African American woman appeared on the far side of bulletproof glass. The officer indicated that she would be my guide. I walked through an hydraulically controlled sliding door into a little room the size of an elevator. After the door had shut completely, a similar door opened on the other side. I was now standing at the intersection of several corridors, each so long it resembled a tunnel. But the thing that surprised me most was the smell. This was a smell that seemed familiar, yet I didn't remember ever smelling it.

I shook the woman's hand and told her my name. Politely, she reciprocated, but other than that she said nothing. We walked along one of the corridors and turned a corner.

As we approached the elevator, we passed four inmates sweeping the floor. They wore orange jumpsuits stamped with RICF in large caps. Three of these young men were Black while the fourth was Hispanic. They could have been young men I saw every day in the City. One of them looked up and seeing my guide tried to persuade her to come over and talk to them.

Three of the inmates were smoking. The fourth stopped sweeping now, pulled a cigarette from behind his ear, and lit up. He flashed a gold tooth with a smile that struck me as both shy and wicked. He took a deep drag on his cigarette. Opening his mouth, he drew back his head as he pushed out the smoke with his tongue, sculpting thereby a perfect ball which hung magically in the air. My guide didn't seem to be looking, but I let the young man know I had seen him; I nodded my approval. Even as I did so, I was aware that it was a slightly patrician nod that had nothing to do with me or what I intended to communicate about myself. I felt as though I had responded from within the role he'd projected onto me, and I stood there confused.

My guide dropped me off at the office where I was greeted by Valerie, the secretary who told me to have a seat. She said the principal would be right with me.

I sat on a bench and watched as I waited. A short White guy in his forties entered the office and joked with Valerie. She called him "Curly." A young inmate was collating some papers at a table. The inmates I'd seen downstairs were wearing orange jumpsuits, but this young man was wearing his own clothing. I later learned that only inmates who had already been sentenced wore the jumpsuits.

"Mr. Trash?" said the voice I'd spoken to on the phone.

"Oh, hi. It's Trask actually. Nice to meet you, Ms. Jaynes." We shook hands. She struck me as a strong woman, well on her way to fifty. She gave my hand a loose shake, but she was very friendly. I followed her into the inner office where I was introduced to another African American woman.

"This is our Assistant Principal, Ms. Cornwell," she told me. "Ms. Cornwell, this is Mr. Trask."

"Nice to meet you," I said. "It's Trask, actually."

"The pleasure is mine," said Ms. Cornwell.

Ms. Cornwell had maybe five years on Ms. Jaynes, but whereas Ms. Jaynes seemed a bit bored, Ms. Cornwell appeared to be fascinated by everything. She looked as if she had dressed for some special occasion. When she shook my hand it was with genuine strength.

"Ooh, I think Mr. Trask is going to be fine, Sharon," she said to Ms. Jaynes. "He's got him a fine, firm grasp. We need more people out here with strong hands."

Ms. Jaynes ignored what I took to be a dig. "Would you like some coffee, Trash?" she asked me.

"No, thank you."

The three of us sat awkwardly on a bench like birds on a wire, I in the middle.

"So," Ms. Jaynes said. "Why don't you tell us a little about yourself."

I told them about my teaching experience, which consisted entirely of college English as an adjunct instructor, about my writing, and various jobs I'd had. I told them that more than anything I was interested in learning everything I could about life because I wanted to write, and it seemed that Rikers had a good deal to teach me.

My soliloquy seemed to bore Ms. Jaynes. She cut to the chase: "Have you ever had a crime committed against you, Mr. Trash?"

I told them about having two bikes stolen, having my apartment robbed, and a car stolen. "But the big one was when one of my sons was mugged. This was when he was on his way to school—he was in middle school at the time. I was really angry about it, but when his mugger was caught and his mother didn't even show up at the police station… I don't know. I wasn't expecting that.

"At any rate, I've spent a lot of time thinking about that kid, wishing I could work with kids in his situation. Matter of fact, do either of you remember a Jeffrey W coming through your school? He's the kid who did it. I was hoping I might run into him out here. He's really…yeah, I guess he's the main reason I'm so interested in taking this job."

Neither of them remembered a student by that name, but they explained that they had a huge turnover of students, many of whom were there for just a few days.

"So you have children," said Ms. Cornwell. "That's great. I think people with children have a big advantage as teachers out here. Because whether we admit it or not, we all know that any day we could get the call that one of our children has been arrested." She watched me closely to see how I'd respond.

I nodded but I was absolutely certain it would never happen to my kids. It would be a long time before I'd be proven wrong.

"If you do decide you'd like to teach here," she said, "I have some strong advice for you: to teach these children successfully, you must forget they're inmates. Think of them as students. Don't ask them about their crimes. Ask about their plans. Don't ask what they've done. Ask what they intend to do. Don't ask about their failures. Ask about their successes, their hopes, their dreams, their aspirations. Their families. These young men love to talk about their families."

"She's right," said Ms. Jaynes. "These kids are kids. Let corrections think of them as inmates."

"To us," said Ms. Cornwell, just shy of interrupting, "they're kids, and as a parent you should try to picture their parents. You should say to yourself every day, 'There but for the grace of God go I.'"

Then they did an odd thing. I couldn't tell if they were confiding in me or what, but they began to speak about God and here we were in a New York City Public School where you do *not* speak about God—especially not the way they were doing it. They said God was working in this school. Ms. Cornwell said it, and Ms. Jaynes agreed. She said she could tell by the change of attitude in Corrections and the students and the staff that God was at work.

After this, they gazed at me and said nothing. I wondered if the talk of God was designed to see if I could be trusted to keep a secret.

They seemed a bit puzzled. On the one hand, I was clearly the wide-eyed White boy Ms. Jaynes had feared I was over the phone. On the other hand...

I still wasn't sure what the other hand was, but I was hopeful that there was one.

* * *

"So you write," said Ms. Jaynes. To Ms. Cornwell she said, "Maybe Mr. Trash could work with Mr. Henie on the journal. Maybe he could start something like that out in the Sprungs."

"That's a good possibility," said Ms. Cornwell.

"I think I'll get Mr. Henie in here and introduce him to Mr. Trash," said Ms. Jaynes.

Ms. Cornwell stuck her head through the door. "Valerie, Dear. Could you send someone to get Mr. Henie."

Ms. Jaynes continued. "You'll be working out in the Sprungs, Mr. Trash. In a few minutes I'll..."

"It's Trask, actually."

"...have someone show you out there and you can follow a teacher around for a day or two until you get used to our routine and see if you like it, Trash."

I was beginning to see this Ms. Jaynes as some kind of Zen trickster who knew exactly what I needed and was pushing my buttons accordingly—Trash Trash Trash Trash Trash Trash Trash.

Someone was knocking. "Come in, Mr. Henie. This is Mr. Trash and we just wanted you to meet him. He's going to be teaching out in the Sprungs. He's an English teacher and we thought it might be nice for you two to get to know each other."

Mr. Henie and I shook hands.

"Jason Trask," I said to him. I didn't want this "Trash" thing getting around.

"How's it going," he said. He was about my age, blond and balding. He looked a little softer than what I imagined one would have to be to do well in a place like this.

"The children love Mr. Henie," said Ms. Cornwell. "They know who cares about them, and he clearly does."

Ms. Jaynes said, "Why don't you explain to Mr. Trash about the magazine you do."

"Well, every month we collect student writing—a lot of poetry, some rap songs, you know, and a few essays and short stories, things like that—and we publish it all in a little magazine."

"Sounds great," I said.

Ms. Jaynes and Ms. Cornwell just watched as we spoke and I had an unfamiliar sense of myself as a White man, a sense I would have frequently during my time on Rikers. I would slowly learn that one aspect of White Privilege is taking your racial classification for granted.

Mr. Henie explained that the high school, RIEF, was divided into two sections. We were in what was called the Building. The other area of the school, the Sprungs, was about half a mile away, and that's where I would be teaching. The kids in both sections of the school were sixteen to eighteen year olds, but the charges the Sprungs kids were facing were not as serious as those facing the building kids.

I felt a little disappointed when I heard that. I wanted the full treatment. In time I would get my wish.

* * *

They asked a Mr. Cumberbatch to walk me down to the Sprungs. As we walked the labyrinthine halls I questioned him mostly to hear his rich accent. He told me he was from Trinidad and that he ran the computer room in the third trailer.

When we came to an intersection, he stopped, remembering he'd left his keys upstairs in the office. He pointed down a corridor so endless its four corners merged into a single point and told me that at the end of it I would find a door on my left. He said I could come back upstairs with him if I wanted, or I could just walk to the end of the corridor and wait there by the door. He would be along shortly.

The place was so intense that the thought of walking down there by myself made me nervous. But I didn't want him to know that.

As I start down the corridor, I grow apprehensive when I see that in fifty yards or so I'll be passing a line of inmates. These guys are adults and they're standing impatiently behind a CO who is smoking and telling them not to.

Several of them see me coming. I realize how scared I must look when I see them pointing at me and laughing.

As I pass the CO, the only white man in their midst, he nods to me as if we're on the same team.

One of the inmates comments about my "skinny white man ass." Another says, "It don't make no difference to me how skinny it is just so it's warm." Someone in the group makes a kissing sound to a round of laughter. Until now, I have not been looking at them as I pass in silence. After a few seconds of this, I begin to feel like a typical, above-it-all White man. I shift my gaze and look at each of them as I pass.

These men look me directly in the eye. I mean directly. They look at me as if they can actually see me. Not the details about me that middle class people use to judge one another—looks, class, intelligence, ethnicity, money, education. There's none of that. These guys are looking deeper than petty details of that sort. In fact, they're looking deeper than my soul. They're looking at my central nervous system—somehow they've hacked their way in and they're examining it through the lens of a single question: how afraid is this guy?

It feels to me that they know more about my fears than my mother does. I look back down the corridor, and as I pass the last man in line he yells to me in white-man-ese: "Well, golly gee; if it's not a representative of the Caucasian persuasion coming to watch the neeegroes work the fields." Then in his own voice he adds, "Welcome to the new plantation, Mister."

3. As Long as My Count's Right

The area of Rikers known as the Sprungs got its name from the tent-like structures the DOC set up after the "Building" was full. Each Sprung was as big as a basketball court and was comprised of a tough, thick plastic outer fabric that was wrapped tightly over a huge metal frame.

There were four of these Sprungs: three housed our students; one, their cafeteria. The school out there consisted of three freestanding, triple-wide trailers. One of them was an administrative building containing office rooms and a large room for faculty meetings. The two classroom trailers each had seven classrooms that I'm guessing were 12 feet by 20. There were four classrooms on one side of a fairly wide hallway and three on the other side. In addition, there was a teacher's room that was more like a closet, and two bathrooms: one for students; one for teachers and COs.

When Mr. Cumberbatch and I entered the second trailer, two White COs glanced over at us from their folding metal chairs. One of them was smoking a cigarette. He sat with his feet on a small rectangular table and his chair tilted back against the wall; the smaller one sat to the side with one leg cocked over the other. They nodded to us.

Mr. Cumberbatch indicated that I should follow him into one of the rooms where a class was being conducted. He introduced me to Mr. Beelman, an English teacher. He was twenty-five, stood six foot eight, and wore nerdy glasses. The kids called him Superman because he was a less handsome version of Christopher Reeves.

We shook hands and he offered me a seat beside him. He was sitting beside the door and behind a desk that formed a barrier between himself and the students who sat facing him. It seemed to me that the teacher who had arranged the furniture in this room—and it was not Beelman—was probably afraid of his students.

Beelman showed me his lesson. He had photocopied an article titled "Bitches 'n Money" from a rap magazine. The article was about how life is more than just those two things. He had several students taking turns reading aloud from it, one paragraph each. Maybe fifteen other students were stationed in the back, some of whom were standing, even walking around. Two of them were stationed by an open window, smoking a cigarette. When

Beelman looked over at them they managed to hide it. One of them saw that I'd seen them. He put his finger to his lips that I should be quiet. I felt no desire to say anything so I just watched. I even wondered if maybe it was all right for them to be smoking in the school. I couldn't imagine Beelman hadn't noticed.

Another kid went over to the two smokers and asked for a hit.

"Yo," said one of the smokers. "Don't be blowin' up the spot." Reluctantly, he gave the kid a drag. Only two or three kids were actually paying attention to Beelman, and they looked like altar boys. They couldn't have possibly committed a crime.

By now I had seen several hundred inmates and except for one Asian, all of them were either Black or Hispanic.

Beelman seemed to have a high tolerance for chaos, but a couple of times the kids in the back of the room began talking so loudly that even he noticed. "Ah, gentlemen," he said. "Ah, excuse me… Gentlemen. Please… Hello, Gentlemen, could you please keep it down?"

"You keep it down, Superman. We trying to conversate over here."

"The word is 'converse,' Gentlemen. As in, 'Converse if you must,' but please keep it down."

One of the smokers imitated him. "'Converse if you must…' Hey, Beelman, where you be gettin' that bullshit at?"

Beelman looked at me. "Word up," he said with a sour grin.

After the period was over, Beelman had a prep period. As we were walking down the hall toward the teachers' room, a kid walked out of a classroom. The smaller CO, a White guy who I would soon find out was well named, asked the student, "Where the fuck you think you're going?"

"I gotta go to the bathroom, Officer."

"You gotta go to the bathroom, ha? Well, boo hoo fucking hoo."

He was speaking with a smile. It was as if he believed he was merely caricaturing a bastard CO rather than being one himself.

"Hey. Listen to me," he said. "Are you paying attention? I don't care if you live or you die as long as my count's right at the end of the day. You got that? Now, get the fuck back in that classroom."

I would hear that CO, Officer Needleman, repeat that line on a number of occasions. He seemed very proud of it. He would later tell me he'd once been a teacher. He said that as a correction officer he made more money and the benefits were better.

*   *   *

After we'd entered the teachers' room, I quizzed Beelman and found he'd been teaching on Rikers for a year and a half. He said it was starting to get easier.

He was not at all what I'd expected of a teacher on Rikers Island. After learning he was a W.A.S.P. from Michigan, he began to make more sense to me.

He told me that most new teachers didn't last very long. Some of them lasted a week; some, a day; some, a couple of hours. Sometimes they'd disappear without telling anyone. The student body was in a similar state of flux. A kid would be in your class for a week and then you wouldn't see him again for a month. Just as you'd forgotten about him, he'd magically reappear and be there every day for three or four months before disappearing for good. Other kids would come in for part of a class, and then disappear forever. Sometimes in the middle of a morning class, an officer would blow a whistle and all the kids would leave and not come back until the following day. Each class was an ever-changing group. A typical class might be seven kids you knew, three you'd never seen, and four who had been missing for several days.

Beelman, who had a keen interest in philosophy, had some good lines. Among them was, "You can't step into the same classroom twice." He said it was nigh impossible to teach in any sort of sequential way. Each day you had to try to build on what you'd done the day before for the kids who had been there, but you had to make it a starting point for the kids who were new.

It was time for lunch. Beelman walked me back up through the labyrinth and down yet another corridor to the lunchroom. Adult inmates stood behind the counter and handed us blue, plastic, "compartment trays" filled with mashed potato, corn, and nasty meat that looked like Spam but was not as good. I sat with Beelman at a table comprised exclusively of Whites. In fact, nearly all of the tables were color specific.

Between teachers and COs the segregation was even more pronounced: I don't think I ever saw a teacher and a CO sitting at the same table unless there were no other tables available. And when that happened, there was always a feeling of awkward separation. From my perspective it seemed as if the COs didn't want anything to do with us, but I suspect they had a perspective of their own.

Mr. Scott was one of the people at our table that first day. He was a short, friendly, southern White guy who seemed genuinely wise—a Jimmy

Carter type. He said that teaching these kids was thoroughly worthwhile. He taught in the Sprungs. There was a middle-aged woman from the building with short, bleached-blond hair who, on this first meeting, seemed a bit cynical about what was possible with these kids. Later I would realize she had a big heart that needed hiding.

Beelman told the story about Needleman not letting the kid go to the bathroom. Ms. Fay, another building teacher, looked as if she might cry when she heard the part where he said, "I don't care if you live or you die…" She'd been teaching there for several years, and said she didn't know how much longer she could take it. In fact, after completing that school year, she didn't return, which was a shame, because she really cared. She pissed off Ms. Jaynes and Ms. Cornwall when the *Village Voice* published her very critical article about her experiences at RIEF.

Near the end of lunch, Mr. Beedy, who later that afternoon would show the video about lions and hyenas, came over and introduced himself to me. He told me Ms. Jaynes had asked him to look out for me. He suggested I hang out with him after lunch and he'd show me a few of the ropes.

Beelman, Beedy, and I walked back to the Sprungs together. On the way I was introduced to several other teachers from the Sprungs. A couple of them told me I was fortunate not to be teaching over in the building where "The Ladies" were. I assumed that to be a reference to Ms. Jaynes and Ms. Cornwell. It was, but it was more complicated than that since no women taught in the Sprungs.[3]

Someone added that Mr. Rhodes looked out for his people.

"Who's Mr. Rhodes?" I asked.

"You haven't met Rhodes yet?" Beedy asked. "He's the assistant principal in charge of the Sprungs. "Shit, why're they always doing that to him? They always stick Rhodes with people and don't even tell him. Don't worry; I'll introduce you when we get back. He's cool, but he doesn't like getting stuck with people he hasn't met."

We walked over to the administrative trailer. "Mr. Rhodes," said Beedy. "The Ladies have been at it again. This is Mr. Trask." And then, imitating the kids, he said, "He a new jack."

Rhodes was unabashedly sizing me up as he listened to Beedy speak. He was a short Black man with an extremely energetic face and body.

"And Trask, here," Beedy continued, "was sent out here and no one even told him that you exist. He was just dropped off out here by who? Who brought you out here, Trask?"

"Mr. ah . . . Shit, what was his name."

"Mr. Shit?" said Mr. Rhodes. "I assure you. There is no teacher out here by that name." He played it completely deadpan.

Beedy laughed. "Yeah, Mr. Shit. He definitely sounds like building material."

I laughed and Rhodes watched me closely. "He was from Trinidad," I said, "and he wore glasses."

"Oh, he means Cumberbatch," said Beedy. Then to me he said, "He's a Sprungs man. He's cool."

"What did you say your name is?" asked Rhodes.

"Jason Trask."

"Well, Trask. Welcome to the Sprungs. It doesn't appear I have a choice in the matter. Either you'll work out or you won't."

"I'll work out."

"We'll see. You have any problems you come straight to me. You don't go bothering The Ladies with anything. Are you clear on that?"

"*Absolutely* clear."

"If you are, then you *might* work out." As he said the word "might" he stood on his tiptoes and lifted his head for emphasis.

"I'll work out," I said.

"Well at least you got you 'n attitude. That's a good sign." When he shook my hand I felt he was testing my strength.

4. Come & Get It

That night all I could think about was what I had smelled and seen and heard and felt out there on that island. First I told my wife about it. When she showed signs of husband saturation, I started calling friends and telling them. Beedy had told me to come up with a lesson for the following day. He wanted me to take a crack at teaching these kids. "You have nothing to worry about. I'll go in there with you," he'd said supportively.

I wondered what I could possibly teach that would hold these kids' attention. I wanted to go neither the Beelman route of boring them all, nor the Beedy route of showing videos. I was determined to teach something meaningful.

That night I stayed up late looking through lessons I'd taught in the past. Now that I'd seen these kids, everything I'd ever taught seemed like a joke. None of it would work out there. And yet I wanted nothing more than to teach these kids. But what did I have to teach them? What did I have to offer? What meaning could they possibly derive from my experience as a White man?

Finally it was approaching one o'clock. I had to get up the next morning at six thirty. I had no idea what I was going to teach. I only knew what I was not going to teach, namely, anything I'd ever taught before. It was so obvious to me that they would see through anything I'd ever done in a classroom that it made me see through myself in a way I found unsettling.

I didn't sleep much. I kept waking and picturing different kids I'd seen out there. At 3:00 I woke up for the last time. I lay there replaying Needleman telling the kid he didn't care if he lived or died. At some point I found myself wanting to do something out there that would change kids' lives. I thought about Jeffrey, the kid who had mugged my son, and I wondered what was going on in his life. He would have been out of jail by now, I assumed.

Soon I was making fun of myself because here I was, completely unable to come up with a single lesson, yet I was going to change kids' lives? I looked ridiculous to myself.

And, by the way, what was that smell out there—why did it seem so familiar?

As it approached six thirty, my anxiety increased. My biggest fear, I began to realize, was not the kids: it was having another adult in the classroom with me. Somehow I felt it would prevent me from being myself. "Okay, then," I told myself. "I'll just tell Beedy I'm going in there alone." After that I felt better, even though I still had no idea what I would teach.

That morning I went around with Beelman again for a couple of periods. Some of the kids recognized me from the day before. A couple of them came over and sat by me. One of them asked me, "Yo, you gonna be teachin' out here?"

"Yeah."

"You teach out in the world?"

I told him about teaching at NJIT. When he heard that I had not been hired back for the coming semester, he smiled. His friend said, "You ain't no REAL teacher."

"I wouldn't go that far," I said. They smiled with me. I thought about telling them about the call I'd received from NJIT the night before, but I knew they wouldn't believe me.

A few minutes later Beedy asked me, "So, Trask. You got something ready? Want to go in there and teach?"

"I sure do," I said. "But you know what I was thinking? I'd really like to go in there by myself."

"Knock yourself out. I just figured I'd take it easy on you the first time. But, yeah… You want to go in there alone, hey… Go for it."

There were no bells to announce the end of the periods, so all of the teachers left their rooms at slightly different times. Two or three of them were standing in the hall with their doors open talking to each other across the hall waiting for the others to finish up. Beedy announced to them, "Trask, here, says he wants to go in there alone."

No one laughed, which surprised me. Mr. Scott said, "That's what I did my first time too. You go in there alone and you're making a statement."

"Yeah," said Beedy, "and the statement you're making is 'Come and get it.'"

We all laughed. Mr. Rafter stepped from the room in which I was scheduled to teach. I asked Beedy, "So I just go in?"

"That's all there is to it," he said. "Until you're in there, that is." He laughed again.

I walked through the door recalling the advice of an old woman who had studied with Gurdjieff in Paris: "When you're nervous," she had told me, "just remember to sense your body—inhabit your entire body, and when you do, you'll feel at home. After all, that's where you've always been."

So as I walked over to the center of the classroom I tried to get in touch with my body. I felt so nervous, I was having trouble finding it.

"How's it going?" I asked them. As I spoke, I could hear that I was breathing funny. My voice had jumped to a higher register. I have always been nervous the first day of teaching a new group of students, but today was different. I felt there was more at stake. So far I hadn't seen anyone actually teach these kids. I had decided not to stay on Rikers unless I could. On my drive in, I had come up with a plan. As I faced my new students, however, I doubted it would work. I had pictured it as a way of getting their attention, and now it seemed silly. But I had to do something. I forged ahead.

There were maybe fifteen kids in there and they were all watching me. Not one of them said a word. They sat expressionless, and I realized they were waiting for me to show my stuff.

I walked over to the blackboard and in one-foot high block letters I wrote, "FUCK."

As I put down the chalk I heard a couple of snickers.

"Anyone know what that says?"

"It says what I'm gonna do to your wife after I get up out this bitch."

He didn't say it like a joke. He said it like he meant it. Everyone was silent and just watched to see how I'd react.

I didn't have a clever comeback and I realized anything less than that wouldn't work. So I just stood there sensing my body.

"Anyone else?" I said.

Another kid said, "It say 'Fuck.'"

"Yeah," I said. "'Fuck.' What have you been taught about that word?"

The first kid spoke again: "It means when you take your dick and you stick it up inside…"

I interrupted him: "Sure, you know what it means. But what have you been taught about it? Is it a nice word?"

"Well, it's nice to do," he said.

"Amen," I agreed. "And most people do it, right?—most smart people."

A couple of them looked amused.

"But what about the word itself," I asked. "Is it considered a nice word?"

No one answered. It was like they suspected a trap. Or maybe they thought that by answering they would be helping me. Why should they

help me? I waited, trying to remember to sense my body. Finally an Hispanic kid said, "No."

"Right," I said. "And why not?"

"It's not polite," he said.

"Okay. It's not polite. But why isn't it polite? What is it about the word
that makes it impolite. We agree—right?—that nearly everyone does it.
And no one says you shouldn't do it, although there are rules about who you
can do it with and when and where. But just about no one has a problem
with a man, you know, like...doing it with his own wife, right? So what is it
about the word that makes it an impolite or bad word?"

"Well, you don't be fucking out in public, so you don't s'posed to be
talkin' 'bout it out in public."

"Excellent point. But what about this word?" I picked up the chalk again
and wrote "INTERCOURSE." I waited. "You guys know this word?"

"Intercourse," a couple of them said.

"Right. Now is that a bad word?"

"No."

"What does 'intercourse' mean?" I asked.

"It mean 'fuck.'"

"Well then why isn't it a bad word too?"

Out of the corner of my eye, I saw Beedy walk past the room, looking in
the window to see if they were feasting on me. But they were all sitting there
listening.

They seemed to be waiting for me to tell them. "You've got two words," I
said, "and they mean the same thing. How does it happen that one of them
is considered a bad word and one of them is not?"

I waited, but no one said anything. I returned to the board and wrote,
"SHIT."

"What about this one?"

"Shit," someone said.

"Is that a good word?"

"Not as bad as 'fuck.'"

"That's true. But it is a so-called bad word, right?"

"Yeah."

"And what about this one?" I wrote "FECES." I pointed at a kid who'd
answered a couple times. "You know that word?"

"No," he said.

"Anyone know it," I asked.

One kid raised his hand. "It says, 'feces,'" he said.

"Right. And what does 'feces' mean?"

"It means 'shit.'"

"Right. It means 'shit,' but is it a bad word?"

"No. It's what the doctor says."

"Perfect. It's what the doctor says. Which by the way is also true of 'intercourse,' right? Okay, so once again, we've got two words that mean the same thing, and one of them is a fine word and the other is quote bad. Why is that?"

When no one answered, I asked, "Are there other words like that?"

In a bit one of them said, "If you call a dog a bitch no one cares, but if you call your girl a bitch, she doesn't like it."

"That's true," I said. "The same word, used two different ways, and it's good one time and bad another time. That's interesting too. It's the same word, but it has two different meanings. And then there are the cases like these words on the board—two different words that have the same meaning and one of them is good and one of them is, quote, bad. Can anyone think of another example like that—where two different words mean the same thing, and one of them is considered better than the other one?"

"Yeah, when you say 'piss,' it's bad, but when you say 'urine' it's not."

"Great. That's the same, exact thing." I stopped to write those two words up there. "So why does this sort of thing happen. Shit is shit, right? Or does it change if you call it 'feces'? And fucking is fucking, right? Or does it change if you say—and here I imitated a Richard Pryor's imitation of a White man—"sexual intercourse." They laughed.

"That's how ya'll White people be saying it."

"Now that's an interesting point," I said. "Do you think that has anything to do with it?"

One of them thought he saw the rule: "Words White people be using is okay, but words that Black people be using is bad."

"Interesting theory. But you know what? This actually predates, that is, it happened before White people and Black people even lived in this country. In 1066 there was this battle in England called the Battle of Hastings.[4] You guys heard of it?"

One kid said he had.

"Do you remember anything about it?"

No response. "The Normans," I said, "who spoke French, took over England. And because they took over, they got all the good stuff and they were the rich people, right? They took what they wanted and the other people, the people who spoke English, became the poor people. And words like 'shit' and 'fuck,' those were English words—they're the words the poor people used. And words like 'feces' and 'intercourse' became part of English through French. And because the people who spoke French had the power, the way they spoke was considered the correct way to speak. And the way the poor people spoke was considered the wrong way. So it's who has the power. That's the way it's always been.

"And it's not only good words and bad words, but it's also true of which grammar is considered 'correct.' The way the rich and powerful and influential people speak is always considered 'correct.' And the way poor people without power and influence speak is considered 'incorrect.' For instance, the Queen of England—she has a lot of money, right? And she may not have much actual power, but she does have influence. Well, the way she speaks is considered correct, right? Does she speak differently from the way you guys speak?"

"She sound like she White."

"Right. For instance, she wouldn't say, 'She sound like she White.' Instead, she would say, 'She sounds like she is White.' Actually, she'd probably say, 'She sounds as if she is White.' So it's like most things. What's 'correct' depends on how you look at it. The fact is, if the Queen of England and all the people with money and influence were to say things like, 'She sound like she White,' then that would be what's considered correct."

"What you teach?"

"English."

"So where you be teachin' out in the world?"

I sat down with them and went through my spiel about having been a college adjunct. And though by now I had in fact been asked to come back and teach, I merely said I was taking this job because my other job didn't have health insurance and this job did.

I asked them their names. One student didn't want to tell me, but the kid beside him told me the kid's name and then his own. We went around the room and everyone else told me their names. After that, we tested my memory to see if I could remember them all. I kept messing up and they laughed at me, but it was good-natured and it felt like things were clicking.

When I got to the guy who wouldn't tell me, I said, "I guess you don't want me to know your name, but I do know it." I moved on to the next guy. The student I'd skipped said, "What my name is?"

"Shawn."

"You only remembered it 'cause I didn't want you to know it."

"Well maybe you didn't tell me so I'd remember it."

Everyone laughed, and he smiled despite himself. "That's that BULLshit," he said. I don't think I've ever seen a more innocent smile.

After that it took me a couple more times around the room before I got all of their names right.

Beedy poked in his head. "Okay, Mr. Trask. The period's over." He checked out the blackboard and looked amused. I said to the kids, "I'll see you guys later."

Several of them mumbled that they'd see me as I started toward the door. Beedy said, "You might want to erase that board." He grinned at me and I erased it. As I was leaving, one of the kids asked me, "What's your name?"

"Jason Trask," I said.

"We can call you Jason?" asked another.

"Sure. That's my name."

I waved and left. "So looks like things went well," Beedy said.

"Yeah, it felt good," I said.

"I just want to give you a little friendly advice," he said. "You shouldn't let these guys know your first name. And you especially shouldn't be letting them call you by it. They'll take advantage if you let them get too close. Not only that, kids get out of here, and when they do, you don't want them looking you up. You should get an unlisted phone number too."

"I don't know," I said. "I've never been comfortable with 'Mr. Trask.' When someone calls me that, I don't know who I am."

"Well what you did at other places, and what you do here are two different things," he said. "I guarantee that out here things are different."

I told him I'd think about it. But I never did.

5. Comfort Zone

When I got home that night, I was overjoyed. I felt confident that I would be able to teach out there. I told my wife all about it and then called the people I'd spoken to the night before along with a few others. Maybe I should have been suspicious of being so happy. Maybe it was simply because I'd managed to solve a problem involving my ego, namely, how to get kids to like me who had reason not to.

As it turned out, my joy was premature.

The next day I spent a period with Mr. Aceves, an English teacher in his late forties. I watched him teach in the most crowded room in the third trailer. About thirty kids were crammed into a space designed for no more than twelve or fifteen. Mr. Aceves let it be known when he entered the room that he wanted to teach, and that he was interested in working with anyone who was serious about learning and that the others should show respect for each other and for those who wanted to learn. He also said if anyone wanted to read, he would furnish books. Three kids approached him, two for books; one to learn.

Aceves had his one disciple retrieve his chair and they pulled out a G.E.D. workbook. The two of them went over some sentences that contained grammatical errors and worked at correcting them. Aceves provided very good explanations concerning why the particular sentences were wrong and what had to be done to correct them.

The other kids talked to each other about all manner of things. They moved their chairs into groups of three and four and spoke fairly quietly. I was sitting near Aceves, which made it difficult to hear entire conversations the kids were having, but I did hear mention of drugs and guns and gangs and a lot of phrases I didn't yet know.

Aceves didn't object except once when a heated argument broke out about whether Sprung One, Two, or Three housed kids with the most serious charges.

Several minutes before the end of the period, Aceves dismissed his student and retrieved his books. As we waited, he said to me, "I've taught in several different public high schools in New York City. This is by far the most difficult. If you're going to teach in a place like this," he said, "it is absolutely essential that you find your comfort zone. It's easy to go crazy out here, because there's so much to be done. If you allow yourself to think about that, you won't be able to stand it. Does this mean you shouldn't care? It doesn't mean that at all. You should absolutely care. But you can never allow your caring to translate into 'I have to educate every one of these kids.' It's great to want that, but the fact is, most of them don't want to change. And that's the reality. It just is. You'll drive yourself crazy if you ignore that fact. Which is why I always say, 'You have to find your comfort zone.'

"Just now I taught one kid. I provided an opportunity for everyone, but only one of them took it, and that's the way it is. I wish they had all said they wanted to learn. But you saw them. They didn't. Probably a few of the others wanted to say it, but they were afraid they'd be made fun of by their so-called friends. The student I worked with is fairly new here, so he doesn't worry yet about being called a 'herb' for wanting to learn. But in a few more days, maybe he will. And depending on the type of kid he is, maybe he'll stop taking me up on my offer to teach him, or maybe he won't. I don't even pretend to know."

I couldn't decide whether Aceves was the wisest man I'd ever met or whether he was copping out. He was a big rugged man who had an extremely kind face and demeanor. I was inclined to believe his philosophy worked for him, but I didn't feel capable of exercising it.

*   *   *

Toward the end of the day, Beedy gave me a crack at another group of kids. Once again I went in there on my own. This time it was a class of about six students. They were all spread across the room and it seemed that the energy was too diffuse. I greeted them and once again I wrote "FUCK" on the board.

One of the kids said, "Oh, he one of them cool niggas." The speaker was a short Hispanic kid with blond hair who was sitting near the center of the room. He laughed derisively—looking right at me. He laughed with everything but his eyes. The other students joined him.

I chuckled, but he saw through it and laughed again.

His dead eyes made him look older. The kids in this school were supposedly between sixteen and eighteen. This guy looked more like twenty-five.

I stood there watching them laugh at me. There was a chasm between us that I thought I'd never be able to cross. The joy I'd felt last night now seemed stupid to me.

One of them said, "White people sure be turnin' red when they mad."

"Word up. That mother fucker is red. Look at him"

"Is you a White man or a red man?"

"I'm a White man," I said, "but we don't choose our race."

"You a corny ass mother fucker," said another.

"He a dumb mother fucker," said another.

The first student, the one who looked older, was now saying nothing. He was simply laughing, proud of what he'd started. He was looking at me as if to remind me that HE was in charge of these students. They were all laughing, and I felt hopeless. It was now clear why this place went through so many teachers. I wondered why I didn't just leave. All of the kids were staring at me as if I were a piece of meat. I suspected that if the COs weren't present, I would literally be dead. I felt like one of those lion cubs in the hyena video we'd seen.

I remembered the old woman's advice about sensing my body, and though it helped some, it also made me aware of the degree to which my body was vibrating with discomfort. For lack of anything better to do, I grabbed a chair, faced them, and sat down.

"We got him under pressure now."

"We got him under MAD pressure."

"Where you be stayin' at?"[5]

"Brooklyn," I said.

"For real?"

"Shit. He prob'ly one of them Bensonhurst niggas." That was a reference to the area of Brooklyn that developed a reputation as a racist neighborhood back in the 1980s when a young African American by the name of Yusuf Hawkins was murdered.

"He probably be lynchin' niggas 'n shit."

"Where in Brooklyn?"

"Williamsburg."

The older Hispanic guy asked me, "Where in Williamsburg?"

Beedy's advice about not even telling them my first name came back to me. I ignored it. "Driggs Avenue," I said.

"Where on Driggs?"

"Just north of Metropolitan."

"I live south of there. I'll be seeing you," he said smiling.

"When you getting out?" I asked. The reason I asked was to engage him in conversation, but as I asked it, I recognized they'd think I was asking out of fear.

They all hooted. Several of them said some version of "He under PRESure."

The older guy answered, "I don't know when I get out. They be layin' more bodies up on me 'n shit, but they can't catch me 'cause I'm too niiiiiice." He hissed the "s" sound for several seconds.

"He don't know the code," one of them said.

"I understood him," I said.

"What he say?"

"He said they keep charging him with more murders, but they can't catch him because he's too tricky."

They laughed again, but this time it had less force. One of them said, "A body ain't a real body. It's a charge. Any charge. We call it a body, but it's just a charge, a crime."

"Shit, don't be tellin' him that," said the older guy.

I said, "Well, basically I had it right, except you're not quite as tough as I thought."

"You sayin' he a herb?" someone asked.

"I didn't say that."

"He don't even know what a herb is," said the older guy.

Another one asked, "You know what a herb is, Mr.?"

I'd already figured out that a herb was someone who was weak. I'd read a *New York Times* article that claimed muggers called their victims 'vics.' I took a stab at it: "A herb's a vic," I said.

"A vic?" one of them said and all of them laughed.

"That's that old shit."

"Vic," several of them repeated as if it were the stupidest word ever.

One of them asked, "You sayin' he a..." He stopped and laughed and said, "...a vic?"

"No. I just thought that when he said 'they be layin' more bodies up on him'—I thought he meant it literally. I'm glad that's not how he meant it."

"Why you glad about that," asked the older guy.

"Well, shit, I mean, if they were trying to lay murders up on you, you'd be like facing a lot of time, right?"

"Yeah. So? What's that to you?"

"Well, I'd hate to see one of my students facing that kind of time."

"Shit. I ain't one of your students. You ain't taught me shit."

They all laughed again and shouted, "Word up."

"But I'm going to," I said.

They reverted to total laugh mode. This time I joined them. I said, "You won't even know about it till it's too late, cause I'm a tricky mo-fo and I'm going to teach you something about English."

"What you gonna teach me?" he asked. Then he said to the others, "No matter what he says, just laugh."

They all began laughing.

I cut through the laughter with, "Well what's that word up there behind me?"

They all laughed.

"What's that word up there?" I asked.

They all laughed.

"Oh, I get it," I said. "You guys are afraid to say it because it's a bad word, right?"

They saw through my bullshit and continued laughing. It seemed pointless. But I sat there and waited.

Finally, one of them said, "You don't have to teach me that word. I know that word," he said, feeling his crotch.

"Yeah," I said. "I'm not surprised you know it. But what kind of word is it?"

They all looked at me blankly? I waited. One of them said, "It's a swear."

"Okay. Now why is it considered a swear, yet 'intercourse' is not considered a swear?" I went over to the board and wrote "Intercourse."

The older guy saw Needleman walk past the window. "I hate that mother fucker," he said.

"Word up," said another. "I see that mother fucker out in the world, I'm puttin' a cap in his ass."

This got them going off in twenty directions. At one point I said, "So why is 'fuck' considered a swear?" They all ignored me and kept talking as though I didn't exist. The older guy grinned at me, reminding me again about who was in charge. I sat back down and just listened. One of them was talking about a White captain who had a tattoo on his arm that was a White baby holding a noose around a Black baby's neck.

"You ever seen it?" I asked.

"No," one of them said. "But what's-his-shit—who that mother fuck-er in Sprung Three who seen it?"

"Perez."

"Yeah, Perez in Sprung Three—he seen it and he told us."

"So why don't you report him—you know, the guy with the tattoo."

"Shit. Don't nobody care about that kind of shit."

"What are you talking about?" I said. "Of course they care. There are Black Correction Officers, right? You don't think they'd care about it?"

"Yeah, but he a captain."

"I saw a Black major the other day," I said.

"Major?'

"Well, yeah. He had an oak leaf cluster on his shirt—a round gold thing."

"He mean a dep."

"Okay," I said, "a dep. It seems to me that a dep must be higher than a captain, right? What does 'dep' mean?"

"Deputy Warden," several of them answered at once.

"Well, yesterday," I said, "I saw a Black dep. Are you telling me that if he knew about this White captain's tattoo, he wouldn't care? Of course he'd care."

"You don't understand how it is out here on The Rock. Ya'll White peo-ple be running this mother fucker, and don't nobody care what some"—he stopped and made his face caricature a White man's— "'neeegro' be saying. It don't matter if he a dep or a dog—don't nobody care."

"Yeah, and besides, you can have any tattoo you want."

"Yeah, that First Amendment shit."

Right after that, one of the COs blew his whistle and the kids went out in the hall and lined up. The only half hopeful sign I received was that one of the kids stayed behind for a few seconds, allegedly to tie his shoe. When he got up, he walked over to me and shook my hand and said, "See you Monday, Mister." I recognized it as an apology.

A few minutes later, Beedy saw me out in the hall. "Didn't look to me," he said, "like you got as much accomplished today as you did yesterday." He grinned and said encouragingly, "The Rock is sort of like everyplace else—sometimes you have a good day; sometimes you don't."

"Yeah... I guess I sort of bombed that class..."

"Sometimes you have a good day; sometimes you don't. It's as simple as that."

As I was getting ready to leave, he told me Ms. Jaynes wanted to see me in the main office. I walked over there and found her.

"How's it going, Trash?"

"Pretty good," I said. "I've taught two classes, and one of them went really well, and one of them...I don't know...it didn't go as smoothly as I'd hoped. But, overall...yeah...I feel like it's going well."

"Well good. I've been hearing good things about you. So are you interested in remaining?"

"Definitely." I said it with such assurance that she laughed, but warmly. I said, "I really love it out here, what can I say?"

"You don't need to say anything. I was just wondering. I'm glad to hear it. I've been hearing good things about you, and I just wanted to let you know. That's all."

I must have looked confused at that point. She said something like, "Well, that was all. I just wanted to see how you're liking it out here, and to let you know I've been hearing good things."

"Well, great. Yeah, I really like it."

"Good. I'll see you Monday, then, Trash."

6. An Arm of the System

All weekend I felt absolute dread of Monday morning.

On the one hand I'd told Ms. Jaynes I loved teaching out there. And when I said it, I was being honest. I loved being a teacher on Rikers.

How was it then that I was so full of dread?

What I hadn't faced yet was that I liked the image of teaching on Rikers. I was teaching criminals. On Rikers Island. Dangerous criminals. Dangerous Black kids. Dangerous Hispanic kids. Kids who mugged people. Kids who sold drugs. Kids who carried guns and knives. And in many cases they'd been engaged in these sorts of activities since they were twelve or fourteen. From what Beelman told me, a couple of our students had actually killed people. And here I was teaching them. I had this naïve notion that all of this made me an exciting guy. A lion tamer of sorts. Not only did I want to look interesting to other people: I wanted to look interesting to myself. Vanity is a mother. And I am her son.

So that was part of it. The part I dreaded is more difficult to explain. It was not only the frustration of not being able to get these kids to do what I wanted them to do. But that was definitely part of it. There was another part that had to do with my admiration of them—and yes, it was on some hopelessly romantic level. Basically it was that these kids do things most people could never do.

Most of us can't just look people in the eye, point a gun at them and say, "Yo, mother fucker, give me your money!" In fact, unless I'm totally pissed off at a person, I can't even say "Go fuck yourself." I'm not built like that. The thing is, my life has been fairly easy. For me, that sort of thing would be like looking at the hand that feeds me and saying, "Fuck you." But the hand that should have been feeding these kids had been giving them the finger. It had left them starving, emotionally, and often physically. In that case, saying "Fuck you" is the appropriate response.

Looked at from that perspective, it's not something to admire, rather something to sympathize with. After all, they were no more responsible for their reaction to what they were presented with than a model boy scout is responsible for helping an old lady across the street. But generally, we admire people who do things that would be impossible for us to do, and that's what was going on in me on some nether level.

These guys had never been reined in, and I admired that because I *had* been reined in. Sure, I'd been kicked out of high school, but since then, I had gradually grown to see the wisdom of caving in. They never had.

And yet here I was as their "teacher" trying to come up with schemes for getting them to cave in. Here I was administering intellectual saltpeter. I was coming to grips with the fact that as a teacher, I was an arm of the system. Whether I was writing "fuck" on the board or telling them it was a beautiful day in the neighborhood, I was still an arm of the system. I wasn't comfortable with this aspect of the job.

I'd had glimmers of this problem every time I'd taught before. Maybe that's what had created the ambivalence that had caused me to leave previous teaching jobs within a few semesters. And then I'd return to word processing for a while—typing documents that helped corporations take over other corporations via leveraged buyouts.

I would word process for a few months and ask myself, "Why am I allowing myself to be part of this?" I'd leave and fall back into teaching. It seemed there was no way I could make a living that didn't involve dirtying my hands.

That weekend, as I considered my job as a teacher on Rikers, a teacher of kids who had managed to live their lives outside of societal bounds, it became obvious to me what it means to have a job as "teacher." It should have been obvious to me all along. The most miserable years of my life were my school years. Summers were fabulous. It was school I hated. I hated it. I hated nearly every day of school from the first day of first grade on. Until college. I loved college.

It wasn't yet obvious to me that the real crisis I was facing was whether to grow up or not. I'd never had a job for more than two years. I didn't want to join the system, but I had taken on responsibilities that required me to have a job. I was married and I had children. No one wanted to publish my novels, so I had to do something.

That second week, we only had students until Wednesday. Christmas was a week away and the coming Friday would be our last day before the break. Corrections worried that the kids would get unruly as Christmas approached. And why wouldn't they? Here they were locked in jail during what for most kids is the happiest time of the year. It's arguable that for many of these students, Christmas had never been a happy time. But one could imagine that most of them had at least received presents of one sort or another, that many of them had enjoyed a great Christmas dinner, that some of them had cherished memories with family. I wondered which of those three groups would miss Christmas the most.

*   *   *

Before we left on break, Ms. Jaynes told me that when we returned, I would be given my own classroom. During the entire break I was nervous. Sure, I looked forward to returning to my job as teacher of dangerous criminals. What worried me was actually doing it. I spent the entire break looking for materials that would hold their interest. I spoke with other teachers I knew, all of whom taught in college, and I invited suggestions. I was looking for a magic formula that would enable me to go in there every day with something that would make them want to learn. No matter what ideas I thought of, none of them sounded right to me. Several nights during the vacation I woke up and thrashed about as I obsessed about these things.

As the end of Christmas vacation neared, this occurred more frequently. I felt unprepared in a way I'd never felt before. The night before I returned to school, I lay in bed agonizing all night long. That last class had sucked the confidence out of me. I kept thinking that if two weeks had produced nothing that they would find useful or interesting, how would I be able to teach day after day. I had come up with a bunch of lessons, but lying there that last night, I knew none of them would work. I felt total despair.

About fifteen minutes after I punched in, I was approached by Danny, a young Haitian-American who had been teaching on the island for several years. He told me Ms. Jaynes had asked him to help me settle into my classroom.

He took me into the room Mr. Aceves had been in when he'd had one student who had wanted to learn. This was the room with the most students in it. None of the other rooms had more than fifteen students in them, but that day with Aceves, this room had about thirty. I later realized that only about twenty-four students were supposed to have been in there. Kids had merely sneaked into Aceves' class.

To me, this seemed like the toughest room. Not only because of the number of kids but because of the types of kids who were in there. In general, they were older and tougher looking than the kids in the other rooms. And they seemed smarter and at the top of the food chain.

Danny told me, "This was Mr. H's room. He was a personal friend of mine, and I'm sorry to see him go. He wanted a leave of absence to go to Puerto Rico to see his father who's dying. Ms. Jaynes gave him a one-year leave of absence a year ago, but when he applied for another one, she said n. He went there anyway, hoping she would give him his job back when he returned. But now it looks like she hired you instead."

He was silent as he opened the locker: "These are your locker keys," he said and handed them to me. "Make sure you lock everything up, even when you're in the classroom. The kids will distract you and steal your shit. You have to realize that. Lots of new people come out here and they are too trusting and they get burned. You've got to understand this. It's just a fact. Even kids who like you will steal your shit. This is a different kind of place. They're in survival mode.

"Also, be sure to count your pencils before you hand them out. Otherwise, they'll take them back to the Sprungs and use them as weapons, stab each other, that sort of thing. And the thing is, if that happens, Corrections will stop allowing us to hand out pencils, which would make teaching out here pretty much impossible. At the beginning at least, keeping track of your pencils is your number one job. Okay, so are you all set?"

I looked around the room and asked him if it was all right if I moved the furniture around.

He said sure. He suggested that I might want to keep it so that I could see every square inch of the room. "Otherwise, kids will be smoking and jerking off and it won't be cool." He handed me a schedule and explained that I would be moving around from room to room. I'd be in this classroom and three others.

I said, "But I thought we teach for five periods."

"We do," he said, "but you'll be spending the first two periods in this room."

"What will I do for two periods with them?"

"The first period we call homeroom, and then in the second period we begin teaching."

"What do we do in homeroom?"

"Just kind of talk to the kids, let them talk to each other, that sort of thing. You're just trying to get to know the kids better during this period and maybe talking with them about things in their world, those types of things. You'll see. It'll work out. Homeroom is great cause it helps you to get to know your kids. But Cornwell wants you to have an aim on the board even during homeroom, so keep that in mind."

I was confused. On the one hand, we could sit around and have a rap session. On the other, we needed an aim on the board. When I asked him about this, he told me I'd see. It would be fine.

He said if I needed anything else, I could ask him or anyone. He left and I walked around the classroom. I knew that in a few minutes the kids would be coming and I was scared. The desk was in the center of the room and I moved it over to the side. I didn't want to sit behind my desk and teach. I wanted no barrier between the kids and me.

To move the desk, I first had to move the locker. I pushed it out of the way and got things settled. Mr. Scott poked his head in and asked if I needed any help. I thanked him and asked him what he usually did with his kids during homeroom."

"I just teach them history," he said. "I spend a few minutes talking to them about things that are going on in their lives, that sort of thing, but when they begin getting restless, I move right into history and give them the same class I give everyone else, but I go into more detail."

I pictured him talking to them about the history of the United States and I had trouble believing they would pay attention. I thanked him and continued to get things set up.

Through the window, I could see across the hall into the room of another teacher, a fifty year old distinguished looking Black man. He was sitting at his desk reading calmly. He clearly was not sweating the fact that in about ten minutes the kids would be arriving. I wondered how long I would be here before I would be as relaxed as he was.

A couple minutes later, Mr. Rhodes entered the trailer and shouted for all of us to come into the hall. We all stood by our doors.

"The students won't be coming this morning," he said. "We'll be having a staff meeting over in the first trailer in fifteen minutes."

I was thoroughly relieved. Maybe something would happen between now and this afternoon that would give me an idea of what to do with these kids.

It wasn't long before Beelman came by to say the kids wouldn't be coming. I told him I'd heard. He said, "No, but not just this morning. They won't be coming this afternoon either."

"Why not," I asked. I was thrilled and sought to hide it.

"Who knows," he said. "Welcome to Rikers."

*　　*　　*

It was the first time I had seen the entire staff in one place. Including assistant teachers and other staff, there were maybe seventy-five or eighty of us. Of the forty or so teachers, twenty-five were from the main building and fifteen from the Sprungs. Over half of the staff was Black, close to a third was Hispanic. With the exception of Mr. Shakir who was from Pakistan, the rest of the staff was White.

For the most part, the building people and Sprungs people sat separately. Each group was further segregated by color. One exception was Mr. Shakir who seemed oblivious to such distinctions.

Ms. Jaynes officiated but Ms. Cornwell did most of the talking. Among other things, she told us that during every period we should have a lesson plan on our desk. In addition, we should have an aim on the board at all times. As soon as we walked into the room, we were to write our name, the date, the subject we teach, and the aim on the board. In addition, the aim should be in the form of a question. At that point she introduced me as a new teacher out in the Sprungs and told me that I should be sure to talk to other teachers about how to form these aims.

Someone asked if we had to write an aim during our homeroom periods and Ms. Cornwell answered, "Homeroom is no different from any other period."

Someone else asked if that meant we were supposed to be teaching our subject area during homeroom, or were we supposed to get to know the kids, which is the way it had always been before.

Ms. Cornwell said that was completely up to us, but if we used it to get to know the kids, we should not simply use it as a time to let the kids do whatever they wanted. We were the teacher and we should be in control of the classroom at all times. Moreover, we should always know what we were going to do ahead of time and have something prepared, even during homeroom. If we were teaching out in the world we would be expected to be teaching, and in here we should be doing the same. That included quizzes and tests and expectations.

Someone said that out in the world, teachers had a static population, whereas ours was ever changing. How could we give quizzes and tests under these conditions?

Ms. Cornwell had an answer: "Teachers are professionals and professionals do not complain. Professionals DO. Professionals take the necessary steps to get the job done. As professionals, you will get the job done as well." She said she was sure we would figure it out. Then she said, "Isn't that so, Mr. Trask."

I smiled and said, "Absolutely," and everyone laughed.

During this entire exchange, Ms. Jaynes looked on with her mouth twisted into a sneer as if she smelled something foul.

She now told us that we would not be seeing the students today because Corrections wanted to keep the kids in the houses. Meanwhile, she said we should keep busy and that building teachers would be meeting over there and Sprungs teachers would be meeting over here.

I was elated to hear Beelman's rumor confirmed. I had been given a reprieve.

*   *   *

Toward the end of the morning, Mr. Rhodes called us to the first trailer for a second meeting. He stood straight, his feet together, his arms at his sides, and he looked around the room at each of us.

When he spoke, he had this way of adding emphasis with his body. A shudder of sorts started at his hips and rippled up his torso to his head. As the ripple rose, he rose with it—he grew several inches in front of our eyes. He would hold this stature for four or five seconds, then drop to his heels and become five foot eight once again. When it came to intensity, he was all Miles Davis; when it came to clothes, he favored Al Green—he loved his sharkskin suits.

He told us something had gone down between The Ladies and Corrections, some sort of disagreement, the details of which he said he could only imagine. He recommended that we show up the next day with a good book: the way he saw it, we wouldn't be seeing our students for a while.

Someone asked, "What, a day? A week?"

"Who knows," he said. "The Ladies begin running their mouths and anything is possible. What they do not understand is we are guests in this House of Correction. We cannot go demanding this and demanding that. Corrections could kick us right the hell out of here and say we are a liability to the safety of this institution. The Ladies do not comprehend any of this. All we can do at this point is sit around and wait."

Someone said, "And get paid to do so!"

"And get paid to do so," Rhodes agreed. He paused and looked us over again. "There is no question, Gentlemen: it is a waste of taxpayers' money and it is a waste of our time. But that is how it is." He stood there watching us expectantly.

"No questions? None? Okay, then. I expect to see all of you looking busy. And 'busy' does not include going outside and throwing the football or playing basketball. The fact is, we do not have students so we must *pretend* to be teachers. And pretend we shall. Am I understood?"

We let him know he was.

As I was leaving, I could feel Rhodes watching me—I was after all the new jack, an unknown quantity. I nodded to him. He barely nodded back.

I returned to my classroom, and spent the half hour before lunch looking through the names of my twenty-four students.

7. Mountain Man

During the next two weeks we had daily meetings of the Sprungs faculty and we hung out in our classrooms. Every day my dread increased. It felt as if I were postponing something I needed to confront, as if I were creating a kind of deficit that would eventually come due. Part of me was disappointed every morning to learn the students weren't coming, but for the most part I felt relieved.

I used the intervening time to develop writing topics I hoped would interest them. Writing was the aspect of teaching with which I felt most comfortable and I decided to make it my focus. I would picture myself teaching these kids. I'd picture them cooperating. But then I'd accuse myself of lying and picture them completely ignoring me. The more I did this, the more I doubted myself, and strangely, the more I wanted the kids to come: I couldn't stand the wait. The disappointment each morning at hearing "Not today," began to outweigh the feeling of relief. Nevertheless, on that third Monday morning when we were told to expect our students, my heart started pounding.

I counted out 25 pencils and grabbed a ream of paper. I wrote the information on the blackboard as we'd been directed. The idea of having an aim felt canned to me, especially in the form of a question. When I start doing things that go against who I am, I get completely lost. The best thing I could think of for an aim was, "How do I write about my life?" As I stood there looking at it, the question felt ridiculous. In fact, my entire lesson felt canned. I knew I couldn't go through with it. But what choice did I have? Especially with my homeroom kids: I had to get through two periods with them. Ms. Cornwall's speech about "professionalism" had me too nervous to just wing it.

As I was looking around the room to see if everything was in order, I heard the students stamping snow off their feet—loudly, in a competitive sort of way. They began moving down the hallway toward their classrooms. Several minutes passed and I was still alone. The only sounds I heard now were coming from the other classrooms; the hallway sounded empty. Just as the hope ran through me of another day without students, a student entered my classroom.

He was a short Black kid. He looked too young to be on Rikers.

"How's it going?" I asked him.

"'S up?" he said. After that, he took a seat and watched me in silence.

"So I'm Jason," I said. What's your name?"

"Metatron," he said. He continued to watch me as if he was determined to figure out what my game was. A couple minutes later, he said, "You that new teacher?"

"Yes," I said.

"Where you be teaching at out in the world?"

I told him about teaching at NJIT.

"So you a professor," he said.

"No. Professors make more money, and they have full time jobs."

"So what are you then?"

"It's hard to explain," I said. "They hire people who don't have PhDs— you know, doctoral degrees—they hire us to teach certain courses."

"So, you a doctor," he insisted.

At the time, I assumed he'd misunderstood me. I would later realize that a lot of kids on Rikers tested people's stories for consistency. They would pretend they believed not the claim you made, but a claim that made you look even better, an improved version of your claim. If you bit, they knew you were not to be trusted. It was a dangerous world they'd grown up in: they were masters at gathering intelligence.

"No, actually," I said, "I'm not a doctor. I only have a master's degree— you know, like most high school teachers."

Another kid joined us. I greeted him and told him my name. He jerked his chin in a subtle nod and told me he was Tyrone.

Three more kids entered and after them another five. I greeted them all, asked their names. A kid by the name of Status came over and shook hands with me. He had a three-step shake similar to one I'd learned in the army. I went with that one and he corrected me. "That shit old school," he said. "This how we be doing it now."

He showed me and I thanked him for the update.

A few more kids came in. "Here," I said. "Let me practice my new shake." I admitted I'd just learned it to gain the trust of the kids who had seen. As I shook hands with Juan and Jamel, I asked my audience if I was doing it correctly. Juan told me Latino kids added a snap of the fingers at the end of the shake, which he demonstrated.

More kids were coming in all the time until nineteen or twenty kids were in my tiny room. I realized that in every classroom, I half expected to spot my son's mugger, Jeffrey W.

One of the kids went over to Metatron who now stood while the two of them went through a complicated shake that included twenty-five or thirty steps. One more kid entered. He stopped by the door and looked at me.

Though he'd never seen me before, he addressed me as if I were a long lost friend: "Mountain man," he said. We all laughed.

"I know you be climbing them mountains," he said.

"Yeah," I said. "I actually do climb mountains."

"And you be eatin' the pussy, too!"

"Oh, yeah?" I said. "What makes you think that?"

"Your beard."

"What's a beard got to do with eating pussy?"

"Eatin' pussy make your beard thick," he said.

"How's that work?" I asked.

He ignored my question. "What's your name?" he asked.

"Jason."

He repeated it, imitating an officious White man: "Jason."

"I didn't say it like that," I said, grinning.

"I did not say it in that manner," he said.

"What's your name?" I asked him.

"Tony."

"So, Tony, am I a mountain man or an 'I did not say it in that manner' man."

"You both."

"AND you be eatin' pussy," said Tyrone, holding his crotch.

"How can you guys tell so much about me?" I said it with a trace of irony, but they did have me curious.

"Cause you White," said Tony.

"So, are all White people that easy to read?"

Several kids answered:

"They faces be gettin' red and you know what they be thinkin'."

"That's how we know you be eating pussy," said Status. "Yo face get red every time we ask."

I said, "What if I'm just embarrassed by the question?"

"Yeah, and you embarrassed because you be doing it," he said.

"What else do White people do?" I asked.

"They be doing all kind'a weird shit."

"Yeah, they be killin' people and eatin' 'em. Niggas be killin' people, but we don't be eatin' 'em."

"Yeah," said Jamel. "We just be taking they shit."

"Word up. White people is freaky."

Suddenly I had an aim I could live with. I went over to the blackboard, erased "How do I write about my life?" and wrote "Why are White people so freaky?" The kids laughed.

"He one of them crazy niggas," said Tony.

"But seriously," I said. "That's not a bad topic. You guys know any weird White people?"

"Who that nigga be eatin' people?"

"Jeffrey Dahmer," someone said.

"Yeah. Now THAT mother fucker—he FREAKy."

"Yeah," I said. "He is freaky. But what about White people in general. Are they all freaky?"

"Not 'they,' said Tony. "You."

"Okay. So are WE all freaky?" I asked.

They laughed as if the answer were obvious—I was the proof.

"Do any of you guys know a White person who's not freaky?" I asked.

Until now, Metatron had not said a word. He sat up and said: "The White man is freaky for one reason and one reason only: and that reason is the White man is the devil."

"Oh, shit," said Tony. "Here he go again."

"I agree with you," I said. "The White man has definitely messed things up, you know? He's enslaved people; he's massacred people; he's polluted the earth, the air, the water. So, yeah, I guess I have to agree with you."

Metatron was silent.

Juan asked, "Yo, Jason. You White?"

"Yeah."

"So why you be dissin' yo people?"

"Well, first of all," I said, "I don't feel connected to being White. I don't think of myself that way."

"You don't think you White?" he asked.

"Of course I'm White. But that's not how I think of myself. When you're Black, you're part of a group that's been pushed around and mistreated. If my great grandfather had been a slave because he was White, and if my father was lynched because he was White, and if...I don't know...if I couldn't get a job because I'm White, you know—if all that were true, then being

White would always be on my mind, right? But the fact is, none of that stuff happened to me. I feel lucky not to have to think about that stuff."

"So you saying you lucky you White?" Tony asked.

"That's not what I'm saying. What I'm saying is…"

"That's what he said." Metatron looked around for support.

"Nigga, you be lyin'," his buddy said to me.

"No, just listen for a second," I said.

"No, *you* listen," he said. "You one of them racist niggas." His anger didn't sound convincing. I decided he was trying to impress Metatron.

Several kids were shouting questions at me, but I locked in on Metatron who asked calmly, "Where you be stayin' at?"

"I live in Brooklyn," I said.

"He one of them Bensonhurst niggas," said his friend.

"No, I live in Williamsburg," I said.

"For real?" It was Tony. "That's where my first baby mama be stayin' at. What street?" he asked. He sounded excited.

"Driggs Avenue."

"Where on Driggs?"

"Between North Fourth and North Fifth," I said. Throwing caution to the wind, I added, "Number 606."

"By that school there?" Tony asked. The excitement in his voice was infectious; it felt like the tone in the classroom had begun to change.

"That's right. Right across from it. But let me get back to what you said, Tony. I need to make a distinction. You know what a distinction is?"

"No, Mr. White Man," he said. "Us niggas don't be knowing them big fancy White man words."

"I'm sorry, Tony," I said. "But I gotta say, there are plenty of high school kids—you know, White kids, Black kids—who don't have a clear sense of the word 'distinction.'"

"Well I'm not one of them," he said.

"Well, that's good. So let me make a distinction: here's the thing: if I hear you correctly, you think I'm bragging that being White is better. That's not what I'm doing. All I'm saying is that if you grow up White, you have it easier. But just because someone's life's easier, it doesn't make that person better."

"All I asked you was do you feel lucky you White. You the one getting all aggy 'n shit."

"Yeah, I hear you, but try to listen *why* I'm 'getting all aggy and shit.' I feel like there's some misunderstanding of my statement—you know, that I feel lucky to have been born White."

Even in that moment I knew I had screwed up: the fact is, I hadn't made that statement. Suddenly I felt I'd lost my footing. This was a place where language mattered.

"How else am I supposed to take it?" he asked.

"If someone didn't know where I was coming from, it might sound like I was saying it's better to be White than Black."

"That's what you said." Metatron was looking serious.

"That's *not* what I said. What I'm trying to say..."

"Oh, what you're *trying* to say," Metatron said and his laughter spread.

"I'm trying to say if you grow up White in this country, your life is easier. Do you disagree with that?"

"Right," he said. "And you said if a person has it easier, that person is luckier."

"Okay, that person is luckier. But his whiteness is not what makes him luckier."

"It's not?" said Metatron, his eyes slit with disbelief. "You just said..."

"Okay," I said. "Just listen. Right now the way our society is organized, it's a person's whiteness that makes him luckier—that's true. But imagine for a moment some other time, some other place where it might be a person's blackness that made him luckier. The distinction I'm trying to make is there are White people—you know, White supremacists—who would say being born White makes you lucky regardless of what else is going on. They'd say just being White is enough, even if people are mistreating you because you're White. That's because they believe Whites are superior to other races. That's not what I believe. And it's not what I said. What I was trying to get across is that being born White in America at this particular time makes it easier for a person to live his life, because White people have the power and unfortunately, they've abused it. It doesn't have anything to do with being White in and of itself. And it doesn't have anything to do with White being better. Do you hear what I'm saying?"

"Yeah, you saying you lucky you White."

"Metatron, I'll hand it to you. You don't abandon your point. You should be a lawyer."

"Yo, mister," he asked. "What's your name again?"

"Jason."

"Jason? That your last name?"

"No, my first name."

Metatron scoffed. He looked around and announced: "He scared we'll find his name in the phone book."

"What are you talking about, Metatron? I just told you where I live. Not only that, my first and last names are up there on the board. Give a cracker a fucking break."

"You mean, 'give a devil a fucking break,' he said."

"Okay, give a devil a fucking break," I said.

They were laughing when Mr. Rhodes stuck in his head.

"How's everything going?" he asked me.

"Good," I said.

"Yo, Mr. Rhodes," said Metatron. "He be saying he glad he White."

Mr. Rhodes looked amused and said to me, "I'm glad you're White too, Mr. Trask." The way he smirked at me as he closed the door made me nervous. I was convinced in that moment that I'd lost his trust. I didn't take him for the sort of man who gave second chances. And yes, I was projecting.

I said, "Come on, Metatron. That's not what I said. Why'd you tell him that?"

"Ooh, now he be gettin' aggy," said Metatron's boy. "We got him under pressure."

"Yeah," I said, "you got me under pressure."

Fearing my sarcasm hadn't come through, I tried to laugh and when I did, I felt my lip curl. That's when I realized how pissed off I was—the students knew it before I did. They were sitting there watching me and grinning. They seemed to think something fun was about to happen, and they were not about to miss out.

It was absolutely clear to me now that I'd never be successful out here. That's what pissed me off most. In theory, this place was a progressive's dream. In reality, it was anything but.

"You guys amaze me," I heard myself say, my voice full of self-pity masked as scorn. "You don't even know who your friends are." Nearly all of them were laughing at me now. At that moment, I had the urge to grab my bag and just walk out the door. I was wondering whether the new semester at NJIT had already begun. If not, maybe those four classes were still available.

My face felt hot and numb. I felt pressure surrounding my body as if I were under water and everything was quiet. The kids were still moving around and I could see them laughing, but I could barely hear them. I pictured the look I was wearing and I remembered teachers I'd had casting that look at me, teachers so repulsive I hadn't even bothered to hate them.

At that point it was clear to me that if I did leave, I would always regret it. I sighed and forced myself to look each of them in the eye. They were watching me. One of my goals had been to get their attention—I certainly had it.

Status suddenly said, "He a red mother fucker," and they all broke into crazy laughter. My face continued to heat up. But not with anger anymore: it was shame for having lost my shit. I didn't know how to react. I'd never been in a social situation that had made me feel like this. I could barely breathe. I was convinced that they would never let me get beyond this moment. I just stood there looking at them.

Before the laughter had subsided, Tony said, "Yo, Jason, what you be teaching?"

"English," I said. I felt grateful to him for providing an opening.

"So," he said. "Tell us for real: you be eatin' the pussy?" The laughter renewed and I felt he'd betrayed me. But there it was again: somehow the laughter felt different. Something had shifted in the classroom. I had a very strong impression that Tony was helping me. Moreover, he seemed to know what he was doing.

I stumbled into the clearing he'd made for me: "Why's everyone want to know if I eat pussy?" I said. "How's that information useful?" I was attempting to smile.

"I'm sayin' though," said Tony.

"You're sayin' though? Now, what kind of bullshit is that? 'I'm sayin' though.'"

Tony was smiling as if he understood my sacrificial treatment of him. I looked around the room and suddenly the laughter felt good-natured. Metatron and his boy were not joining in—I hadn't fooled them. Seeing the looks on their faces, it was clear—my trial had not yet ended. I suddenly felt exhausted. I couldn't take another round of this.

I chose that moment to hand out paper and pencils. Even as I was handing them out, I didn't know what I was going to have them write. It would be ridiculous to assign the lesson I'd planned—write about your earliest memory.

"What's this bullshit?" Tony asked, when I handed him the paper.

"This bullshit, Tony?" I said. "This bullshit is what is known as paper. I can't believe you: you know the word 'distinction' yet you don't know what paper is? Now that I find interesting."

He was grinning.

"So," I said, "we just had a conversation about being White versus being Black. I said it's easier to be White in this society because of all of the prejudice that exists."

"You didn't say nothing 'bout no prejudice," Metatron said.

"Sure I did. I talked about the White man abusing his power. I talked about the White man enslaving Black people. Now, just because the word 'prejudice' doesn't appear in those statements... I mean, come on, Metatron. It's pretty clear: I was talking about prejudice."

"Now you changin' it," he said.

"How'm I changin' it? I also talked about if my father had been lynched."

"But you didn't say nothing 'bout no prejudice," he insisted.

"Okay, Metatron, so let me ask you this: if someone owes me seventeen dollars for a pipe and thirty-five dollars for a bag of weed, how much does he owe me?"

"Fifty-two dollars," he said without even thinking.

"But wait a second," I said. "I didn't say nothing about no fifty-two."

"No, but you..." He stopped and smirked at me.

"Exactly," I said, and I practically yelled it. "I didn't use the word 'fifty-two,' but we all knew I was talking about 'fifty-two.' And just because I didn't use the word 'prejudice,' the fact is, I was talking about 'prejudice.' Everything I said added up to prejudice." I glared at him, gloating at my win.

It hurts to admit that I was trying to shut him up—stamp out his voice. He met my look with the blankest face I've ever seen—no affect whatsoever. Everyone was quiet. Suddenly aware that I was being an asshole, I softened my gaze, and at that moment he looked away.

"Let me get back," I said, "to what I was saying earlier: it's easier to get by in this society if you're White. But I don't know that. Because I've never been Black. And you don't know it because you've never been White, right? So what if some White guy suddenly turned Black? You know, like, what if I suddenly turned Black? What kind of advice would you have for me? That's what I'd like you to write about. What advice would you have for me if I turned Black?"

"You don't have enough paper to write all you need to know."

"Word up. Ain't enough paper on Rikers Island."

"Ain't enough paper in this motherfuckin' world."

I said, "You don't have to tell me everything. Just give me a few pointers, you know? Help me survive. Give me some advice."

Several kids began writing. To the others I said, "What are you waiting for?"

"I wouldn't write you," one of them said. "I'd tell you."

Others agreed.

"How about this?" I said. "Just give me five pieces of advice. Just tell me five things I need to know. You know like, 'Make sure you do this,' 'make sure you don't do that.' Things like that."

"Make sure you don't have a heart attack," said Rodney, "when you see how big yo dick is." Now they were all laughing. Everyone laughed—even Metatron looked like he might join in.

"I'm not lying," said Status. "My shit's big."

"First time you pick yo shit up," said Tyrone, "you probably drop that mother fucker, it so heavy."

They were all suffocating with laughter.

"So that's it?" I said. "That's your advice for me as a new Black man. Here we were talking about how there's more suffering when you're Black. Are you're telling me it's because you have a big dick? That's it?"

"Damn straight. That shit be mad heavy."

"That's why Five Oh caught me. I tripped over my dick," one of them said to an encore of laughter.

"Okay," I said. "I guess if that's your primary piece of advice, write it down. What's your second piece of advice?"

Metatron raised himself in his seat and raised his hand to get my attention: "Yo, Mister," he said. "Why you having us write this bullshit for? You just be defiling niggas and making fun of 'em and making 'em look like they stupid."

"I'm not defiling *any*one," I said defensively. "I'm trying to get you to write. I believe writing is a purifying act. It doesn't matter what you write about. If you get yourself into the habit of writing, especially about your feelings and thoughts, it clarifies your thinking and something happens. So I'm doing what I can to get you writing. Because I think it's going to help you know yourselves better. And if you don't buy that, fine. But you have to admit, if you can write well, you'll be eligible for better jobs."

Metatron had made his statement and he had nothing to add. I don't think I ever admired a student any more than him. Most people have to keep arguing their point. I know I do. Metatron believed what he said and whether you agreed or disagreed, it didn't matter to him. He knew he was right. His confidence was unsettling. I wanted to keep arguing to convince him, but he wouldn't give me that. He sat back and shut me off.

A number of the kids had written about how burdensome their appendages were. Several read me their advice.

"Okay," I said. "What's another piece of advice you have?"

"Now you can jump." It was Rodney again.

"Now I can jump?" I said. "Come on! You claim it's more difficult to be Black than White, right?"

"No, that what you claim," he said.

"Oh, so it's not harder? Look around you. How many White kids do you see in this classroom? Are there any White kids in the whole Sprungs?"

"Before Christmas there was a White kid in Sprung Two, but he gone already."

"Where'd he go?" I asked.

"His mom bailed his ass out."

"So why do you think there are no White kids in here? Don't White kids do crime?"

"They be doin' crime, but they don't get arrested."

"And when they DO get arrested, they get bailed out."

"And if they DON'T get bailed out," said Tony, "the judge be givin' 'em breaks. 'Young man, seeing you are Caucasian and all, we are going to pay you three thousand dollars for your inconvenience. We know it was some nigger who done the crime.'"

"So if that's what you believe, why not advise your new Black man to get used to being treated like shit. Why are you saying 'now you can jump' when there are important things I need to know? Try to be serious."

"How we supposed to be serious? You ain't gonna turn Black."

"Word."

"But what if I did?" I asked.

"You won't."

"You guys heard of that book *Black Like Me*? The author had his skin dyed black so he could feel what it was like to be discriminated against."

"That ain't being Black," Tony said. "Black ain't just a color. Black is something inside you."

"Yeah, ain't nobody Black unless he born Black."

There was some commotion in the hall. I looked up and realized the other teachers were ready to change classes. We'd gone through two periods—homeroom and period one. I collected their papers. Only about nine kids had written anything besides their names.

I had a more difficult time collecting pencils. At least a fourth of the kids claimed they'd never received one. Tony said, "Just give the man his fucking pencils." After that, they cooperated.

As I erased the board, Juan asked if I was going to be their teacher every day. I told him I was. No one said good or great or anything like that. I was just happy no one complained. I moved toward the door for my next class.

"I'll see you guys tomorrow," I said.

A few of them said something like, "Okay, Jason" or "See ya." Jamel even said, "Thanks, Jay."

Metatron was sitting by the door. As I passed him, I tried but failed to catch his eye.

Hoping to patch things up with him, I said, "Take care, Metatron."

He scoffed: "Don't be trying that devil shit on me."

I said, "What do you expect from the devil?"

"I don't expect nuttin' from the devil," he said, "and that's what I got."

8. Nasty, Short & Brutish

I met with the next group for only one period, the first half of which seemed as long as the previous two periods. There were only about eight kids in the room and most of them seemed sleepy. I tried to get a conversation going that would lead to the writing assignment I'd given the previous class. They showed no interest. I kept trying to force the issue and nothing happened. They just sat there, six of the eight with their heads on their desks. They had no interest in what I was selling. And then I asked the obvious question, "Why are you guys so tired?" After that things picked up.

One of them said, "Cause the turtles be comin' in and fuckin' with us."

"The turtles?" I asked.

"Yeah, them mother fuckers in them turtle looking suits with them big-ass clubs."

"What do you mean, turtle looking suits?"

"Big ass padding and helmets and them face shields."

"Who are they, COs?"

"Yeah, but they be special trained to be mean."

"They big mother fuckers and they be fuckin' niggas up."

"How come the kids in the next class over weren't tired?"

"They not in our sprung."

"So why'd the turtles come to your sprung?"

"Cause three niggas got cut."

"What do you mean, cut?"

"You know, with razors."

"With razors? Where'd they get razors?"

"To shave with. They be givin' us razors to shave with and niggas be breaking out the blade and puttin' it in they mouths."

"In their mouths? What do you mean?"

"They take them Bic razors, and they break out the blade and slide it right here." He indicated between his cheek and teeth. "They leave it there all day until they need it and then they be spittin' out on niggas and cuttin' 'em and then they put the blade back in they mouth."

"You're kidding me."

"Johnson, show him your scar," one of them said.

A kid with a shaven head leaned his head forward and showed me a five inch scar across the back of his neck, half an inch wide and raised.

"You got that here?" I asked.

"Yeah."

"Did you have stitches?"

"Yeah."

"Did it hurt?"

"No. I thought he missed. You know, I felt his hand touch me, but I thought the razor missed. Then I felt up there and it was all bloody and shit and I'm like damn. Nigga got me good."

"So why'd he do it?"

"Cause I deaded him for his shoes when he first came."

"You 'deaded' him for his shoes? What's that mean?"

"New niggas be comin' in and niggas be taking they shoes 'n shit."

"And you call that 'deading' them for their shoes?"

"Yeah."

"So since then, have you deaded anyone else of their shoes?"

"Not shoes, but I deaded a nigga for his jacket." He looked over at a smaller kid. The smaller kid grinned sheepishly. Everyone teased him.

"So that jacket you're wearing right now, is that the jacket?"

"Yeah."

"So that's not your jacket?"

"It is now."

"What do you mean, it is now?"

"It's my motherfucking jacket."

"How do you figure?"

"Cause I took that shit. Possession—that's nine tenths of the law." He grinned.

Another kid said, "Yo, Jason. That's how things be workin' in here. Niggas got to know that when they come here. Shit's real up in here."

"But do you like getting your clothes taken from you?"

"Hell, no," said the kid who had taken the jacket.

"Then why do you take other people's clothes?"

He grinned. "People be doin' that shit to me," he said.

"Any of you guys ever hear of the social contract?"

No one responded.

"The social contract is an agreement between people that's something like, 'If you don't take my shit, I won't take your shit. If you don't kill me, I won't kill you. If you don't take my woman, I won't take yours,' you know? It's an agreement. And this philosopher guy Thomas Hobbes said that without that kind of agreement, 'life would be nasty, short and brutish.' You know that word, 'brutish'? It's from the same word as 'brute.' So 'brutish' means 'like a brute,' you know. So essentially, Hobbes is saying, if we didn't have this agreement among people not to mess with each other, life would be nasty, and short, and like living with a bunch of brutes. Wouldn't you rather live under some sort of agreement like that?"

"That shit sound boring."

"So you like getting scars across your neck?"

"No. But niggas don't be slicing me no more."

"Not now, but you keep stealing people's shit, and they're going to get back at you."

The whistle blew signaling that the kids should line up in the hall.

*   *   *

That afternoon I met two more groups. The last one was the first class I'd taught, the one that had gone well when I'd written "fuck" on the blackboard. In both of those classes we had a good discussion, but we never got around to doing any actual schoolwork. Despite that, at the end of the day when it was time to leave, I was feeling good. I was getting to know the students I would be working with every day, and it seemed to me that I would be able to handle it just fine. That night was the first night I slept well in a couple of weeks. I didn't wake up even once to worry about what I was going to teach the next day.

*   *   *

By now I had begun to realize that I would probably never run into Jeffrey out there. And the thing is, it no longer mattered to me. I no longer felt the need to find him in order for teaching out here to be a meaningful experience. The place was full of Jeffreys.

That next morning I went in confidently, prepared for things to go my way. But instead of having classes, we were told that the new captain wanted to speak to the Sprungs teachers.

The Sprungs teachers gathered in the first trailer and in walked a short, intense, angry White guy. He stood like a short kid standing next to a tall kid, his chin up to make himself appear taller.

"Good morning," he said. "I'm Captain Rizzo, and I'm taking over control of the Sprungs. I think it's great that you want to come out here and teach our kids and I want to make sure things go well between us. You do a difficult job out here and I just want to assure you that I'm aware of that. We also have a difficult job to do and we do it very well. And I want to make sure you're aware of that.

"You'll soon see I'm a guy who does not mince words. I'm going to say a couple of things and I'm going to say them bluntly. I'm not trying to be rude; I'm just trying to be clear. So please listen. The main thing I want to say should come as no surprise to you. You are here to teach these kids. And that's it. End of story.

"You are not here to be their counselors. You are not here to be their parents, not their *brothers*. And you are not here to be their friends. You are here to teach them. Period. I trust all of that is clear to everyone. Because if it's not, I want to know right now. I want to know if there's anyone here who doesn't understand what I'm saying because if there is, I need to talk to that individual to clarify a few things. Teach the kids. God knows they need to learn. But you need to learn too. And what you need to learn is that you are visitors in the House of Corrections. This is my house. And as long as you are clear about that fact, everything ought to go just fine. If you're not clear about it, things won't go fine. You with me?"

Most of us nodded or murmured assent.

"Excellent," the captain said. "That's all I wanted to say. Are there any questions?"

Dr. Steele, the fifty something year old relaxed Black man whom I'd since learned was a retired lawyer, asked, "Is there some particular reason that you're telling us this now? What I mean is, did something happen or is there some specific thing that we should do differently?" He asked it politely, but a sense of independence was present in his voice that I'm sure the captain picked up.

"Excellent question," the captain said, and he looked down. He looked up again and spoke more loudly: "What you should *all* do differently is understand that you are visitors. When you're in my house, you don't treat it like it's your house. You are to act like guests. So you should all do that part differently. If there's a fight in your classroom, you need to alert an officer and trust him to take care of it. You don't get paid to break up fights. We do. If you hand out pencils, be sure to get them back at the end of the period. In the hands of an inmate, a pencil is a very effective weapon. And it's a weapon a metal detector won't pick up. We don't need kids traveling around with weapons on their person. So when you hand fifteen pencils out, get fifteen pencils back. If a kid doesn't hand his pencil back to you, tell an officer. If you don't know who has the pencil, tell an officer. That's why we're here. Is there anything else?" He waited, moving his head around in sudden, sporadic, birdlike movements. No one said anything so he thanked us, Mr. Rhodes thanked him, and he left.

Mr. Rhodes was silent as he stood before us and waited for the captain to leave. After we heard the outer door close, he said, "I'm glad The Ladies were not present for that presentation or they would have had something to say and things would have gotten out of hand. So if you do not like what you just heard, that is fine. We can talk about it now. But whether we talk about it or not, I want all of this to stay here and not end up getting leaked over to The Ladies." He looked around at each of us to make sure we understood.

Several people spoke about how they preferred the last captain who while he had been firm, had managed to be laid back unless it was necessary to come down hard. Dr. Steele said he suspected that if we cooperated with this new captain and made him see that he had nothing to worry about from us, in time he would come around. Mr. Scott agreed with Dr. Steele. He said when the old captain was new he had been far less laid back.

Mr. Beedy said, "We definitely don't want The Ladies to know about this because they would feel the need to make the captain understand that we have a right to be here too, and sure'n shit, that would lead to us not seeing the kids for another two weeks." He went on to say, "If anyone in the building hears about the captain's speech, The Ladies will find out too—that's just how they are over there—doesn't make any difference if we tell women or men, that's just how they all are."

Before he dismissed us, Mr. Rhodes told us that we wouldn't be having students this morning because the captain also wanted to speak to them to orient them to his new rules and ways of doing things. And that was another thing he didn't want reaching the building.

"So this morning, what I want you to do is look busy. And until it is time for lunch, do not be going over to the cafeteria and hanging out. And when lunch time is over, head on back here and look busy again. Because

I suspect we will not be seeing the students this afternoon either."

As he dismissed us, he stood by the door and looked each of us in the eye as if to remind us that we had taken some sort of solemn oath. We all went to our classrooms and hung out in them.

9. Real School

I found a couple of magazines of student writing that Mr. Henie had compiled. They contained poems by our students about what it was like to be in jail, how hard it was to be out there on "The Rock." There were letters to their babies about how badly their fathers had screwed up, how they were going to change their lives and bring up their kids so they didn't have to go to jail. Some of the writing was good.

Mr. Malcore, who had a classroom next to Dr. Steele's, came over and introduced himself. He was a fairly tall guy with reddish hair and he always wore a coat and tie. He was a science teacher who had grown up in Oklahoma. He told me that Ms. Cornwell had asked him to come check up on me and make sure everything was going well and that I had everything I needed. We had a conversation about teaching these kids. He had been teaching there for five years and really liked it. He didn't know how much longer he would stay with it.

After that, I went over to see Mr. Scott. I sat down on a table while he rummaged around and organized things in his closet. He showed me some of the things he had that were nearly impossible to get out here such as a screwdriver. "If you need one of these for any reason, let me know. But not when students are around. If they found out I have it, some of them would do anything to get it. Not only that, one of them might tell corrections about it and then they'd take it because it's a potentially deadly weapon."

He told me he liked to travel with his wife, and that every summer they took a long trip around the country to look at historical sites and whatnot. I must have stayed in there for over an hour because suddenly he asked me if I was going over to lunch.

As we walked over to the cafeteria Beelman joined us. I was feeling strange by now about the fact that though more than half of the faculty was Black, I was always with White people. None of the other teachers seemed to mind or even notice—they were all with their own kind as well. To me it signaled that something was wrong.

We sat with Ms. Fay from the building. Everyone asked what I'd been doing with the kids in class. I told about talking with them about the turtles and kids getting "deaded."

Scott said, "They love to talk. You can have great conversations with them. When I was in your shoes the difficult thing was getting them to do schoolwork."

I nearly told him I'd seen great teachers for whom talking *was* the school-work. Realizing I was being defensive, I admitted that it was my difficulty as well. I told about handing out paper and pencils in the first class and trying to get them to write but only a few put in any effort. He said it brought back memories.

Ms. Fay said she'd had a lot of trouble getting the kids to do work for her when she'd first come as well. Beelman said he still had trouble with it.

Mr. Scott gave me this advice: "The main thing is you have to keep hanging in there and someday soon something will happen and your students will start doing your work. There's a chance you may not even know what you're doing differently. As a matter of fact, I doubt if you will be doing anything differently. But you'll be feeling differently and they'll pick up on that and respond to it."

After lunch, I decided to try to broaden my list of acquaintances on the island. I went over and introduced myself to Dr. Steele. He was an impressive man. He had this gentle quality about him that rested securely on a foundation of strength. He told me he had retired from his legal practice. Now he was sharing what he'd learned with the kids.

He taught them street law, the sort of law they would need in order to survive back in the world. Ethical issues. Issues about their rights, about housing, searches and seizures, arrests, driving, legal issues that would arise when they got jobs. He also taught them the legal terms they would need to know in order to understand their cases. He told me that kids sometimes brought up things in class that their lawyers had told them, or they'd show him papers they had received from the court, things they didn't understand. Steele would explain all of this to them.[6]

When I got home that day, I had a funny feeling I would have frequently during the remainder of my time out there, a feeling that had to do with the radical difference between my life and the lives of my students. I could leave every day and they were stuck there. Not only that, my entire life had been easier than most of their lives had been.

*   *   *

A couple days later at lunch, I mentioned again my issue of not being able to get the kids to write. Ms. Fay said that when she'd first started, by talking to the kids about what they had done in school back home, she realized what the problem was. The only teaching most of them had ever experienced was worksheet teaching. When they got a blank sheet of paper and were asked to write about their lives or to answer an open-ended question, it didn't seem like "real school" to them. She suggested that if I were to do the worksheet routine for a couple of weeks, they'd get used to working for me and then slowly I could introduce something more meaningful and they would do that as well.

That night I went out and bought a couple of workbooks containing grammar exercises. I chose an exercise about subject / verb agreement, photocopied it and brought it in the next day. I did a lesson explaining that if you used "and" between two subjects, the verb should be plural, but if you used "or," the verb should be singular, unless both subjects or the subject closest to the verb was plural. I wrote several examples on the board and had them tell me what to write. After they understood it, I handed out the worksheets and sure enough, all but one of my students that day answered the questions.

During the previous class, I had asked them to write a page about what they were going to do when they got out of jail. Several students in each class had taken it seriously, but the great majority had written only a sentence or two. One kid had written, "Yo, Jay, when I get up out this mother fucker I'm gonna rape your wife and your dog." Coming from this particular student, I knew it wasn't an actual threat. This was his sense of humor at work. The thing is, he had clearly not taken the assignment seriously.

But now, seeing a worksheet in front of him, he, and nearly all of his classmates, appeared compelled to finish it. If they made the slightest mistake they wanted White Out to correct it. An eraser wasn't good enough.

Anyone who has ever worked with gifted children knows that they are often total perfectionists. That's how an amazingly high percentage of the Rikers kids were. And if they didn't know a single answer to a question, they whined about how difficult it was and they'd ask for hints. I was horrified. I'd respected them more when they refused to do the work. What got to me most was that they thought this was "real school" and that the writing exercises I'd had them do earlier were something that a "real teacher" would never have students do.

That afternoon as I walked the long hallway from the Sprungs to the check-out site, I noticed the smell of the place for the first time in several weeks. At once I recognized why it seemed so familiar: it was the slightly chickeny smell of human beings. The place was never aired out so the smell was intensified to the point that it seemed unfamiliar. I realized that what I was smelling was what a human barn would smell like. That moment had a profound effect on the way I saw Rikers after that—more than ever it appeared like a plantation to me.

*   *   *

That night as I went over the worksheets, I was amazed at how well the kids had done and how much effort they had put into them. The next day as soon as I walked into each of the classes they asked how they had done. "Did I get a hundred, Jay?" Kids walking past my classroom to the bathroom even stopped to stick their heads in my door to ask me.

I had them do worksheets for a couple of weeks and then I gave them a hand-out that I word processed in such a way that it looked like a worksheet. At the top I had written an open-ended question that called for a paragraph about a life mistake they had made. Beneath it, I included lines for them to write on. I had already discovered that they hated to write on blank paper. They wanted lines, god damn it. This time they all took it seriously and I received some really good pieces of writing. Nearly everyone wrote something resembling a paragraph, and some filled the entire page.

10. How to Steal a Lexus

I may have been a teacher out there, but I learned at least as much as I taught—mostly about myself, but not only.

I would sometimes tell a story about an experience I'd had as a way of getting them to tell stories about their experiences. The hope was that through this, they would realize they had experiences worth writing about. The favorite topic of the students in one of my classes concerned stealing cars.

There were very few kids out there who had been arrested for stealing cars, though many considered it a sub-specialty. When things were slow, it provided cigarette money. They would tell about going out and finding the car they wanted. One such story I remember included the trick for disabling the alarm system on the Lexus. I assume that by now Lexus has remedied the problem so I don't mind sharing it. And please note: I have never tried any of this stuff, so please don't take my word for it.

Though the Lexus was "theft-proof," the kids claimed it was an easy car to break into. They would take a powerful magnet from a huge loud speaker and attach it to the frame of the car. They'd leave it there for half an hour or so. By the time they came back, the magnet would have fried the alarm system's chip.

After that, they'd take a dent puller and pull the keyhole out of the car door. They'd stick a finger into the hole, open the door, and get in. Once inside the car, they would use the dent puller to pull the ignition keyhole out which gave them access to the wires. They'd touch the wires together until the engine started. They would have brought a crowbar along with which to snap the steering wheel lock and off they would drive.

My students laughed when I told them I had "The Club." Urban drivers are familiar with this anti-theft device that attaches to the steering wheel. Because one end of the club is so long, turning the steering wheel becomes impossible. But according to my students, removing The Club was no problem whatsoever. They would spray it with Freon, which would make it incredibly brittle, and then they would smash it with a hammer. They claimed all respectable car thieves carried all of these tools in their bags.

In other cases they would encounter a car from which the entire steering wheel had been temporarily removed by the owner. At least one company made removable steering wheel kits designed to prevent car theft. My students always carried a pair of vice grips which they would attach to the nut in the center of the steering column, and they'd drive with their vice grips as an *ersatz* steering wheel.

When they'd talk about this stuff, they'd get incredibly excited. It was as if we had at last lighted on a topic that had meaning. The car thieves were proud of what they knew. One of them would talk about how to break into a certain model of Ford, say, and another kid would correct him about some esoteric detail.

But for the most part, they rarely disagreed with each other. It was as if they'd been reading from the same guide. Even kids who weren't car specialists knew an amazing amount about stealing cars. You never knew when you'd need to steal a car, so it paid to know these things.

They'd also talk about the business end of car thievery. In most cases, unless they simply wanted to go joy riding, they would take the car to a man they knew who would give them cash. Depending on the car, the price varied, but two hundred dollars seemed typical. Some of the kids actually worked for these men. Not only would they sell them the cars they stole, they would also strip them down to the quick. Later those parts would either be sold or recombined with other parts to make new cars out of several stolen cars. Sometimes they'd get orders for several of the same make, year, and model. There would be a competition to see who could get the most cars.

My students would tell about how scared and excited it would make them to approach a car and try to determine whether anyone was watching it. Most of them would then leave the car for a while and watch from a distance to see if anyone had noticed. Later, they'd approach it again and look inside the car to see if anyone chased them off. If not, with dent puller in hand, they'd approach the car, unless, of course it had an alarm. If it did, the first step would be to disable the alarm, or maybe break in anyway, depending on the type of alarm it was, how good it was. Some alarms shut off as soon as you started the engine. All of the kids claimed that the process from starting the break-in to driving away in the car would take a little more than a minute. If everything went well, less.

After I'd been teaching there for six months or so, I'd find myself out walking my dog at night passing parked cars and I'd be wondering what it would feel like to look at a car with the intention of stealing it. I couldn't imagine it. The act screamed against everything I'd been taught. Then I would try to imagine myself past that hurdle to see what it would feel like to actually break in and take it.

I couldn't do it. I realized that even if I could talk myself past my conscience, I had an unbelievably huge fear of getting caught. I'd be thinking about how if I got caught, I would lose everything. It was a reminder that I did not possess free will. If I had free will, it seemed to me, I would at the very least be able to imagine stealing a car, but I couldn't even do that—not in any authentic way.

Then the question arose, do my students have free will? Was it free will that enabled them to take the car? I had trouble believing it was. From what some of them told me and from the writing of others, many of them had never actually been taught "right" from "wrong." For those kids, stealing did not go against what they'd been taught.

How could a kid who had grown up like that be held accountable in the same way as someone who had two parents who had taken pains to teach him not to steal the property of others.

I also remember walking my dog at night up toward Greenpoint where I would often run into drunk men. They would be stumbling around, completely confused. Knocking them down and taking their money would have been incredibly easy, or so it seemed. But I was always aware that my thinking was simply academic. There was no way I would ever be able to go through with that sort of thing. My past was too strong. My parents' teachings were too strong. Even as a kid I couldn't go into a store and steal a piece of penny candy. Such an act was beyond me. I could rebel against the lesser rules, but I had no option to go against the basic, foundational laws.

Most people believe themselves good because they don't kill and rape and steal. The fact is, most law abiding citizens would not be able to kill and rape and steal even if they wanted to. And since that is so, their behavior has nothing to do with being good. It's merely the result of positive brainwashing of a sort that was absent from the upbringings of many of my students.

One day I told the kids about my experiences with eying cars and drunk men. This excited them. I realized at once that they thought they were witnessing the criminalization of a teacher. I told them I couldn't possibly do it.

They said I was just scared.

I admitted that was true, but that even before I got to the hurdle of my fear, there was another hurdle, namely, the hurdle of my conscience. I explained that I was incapable of even contemplating with any degree of seriousness the taking of someone else's property.

They said, "Haven't you ever shoplifted?"

I said no.

They had trouble believing this. They recited cases of movie stars with tons of money who had been picked up for shoplifting. They assumed everyone shoplifted. When I told them I never had, they said I was lying. That prompted one of them to ask me: "Yo, J-Dogg. If someone was to give you a million dollars for killing someone and you was sure you wouldn't get caught, would you do it?"

I said, "No."

They all said, "Bullshit."

One of them then asked me, "Okay, so if you're so good and so honest, why was you thinking about stealing a car and mugging someone?"

I tried to explain to them that it wasn't that I'm so good and so honest. It simply had to do with the way I was brought up. In trying to picture what it would be like to do those things, I was simply trying to understand them, trying to understand what it was like to be them at the moment they committed their crimes. But I was completely aware that I really couldn't even do that.

They told me I was fooling myself, that slowly I was losing all that stuff that kept me from stealing and soon I'd be doing it too.

I began to feel I'd made a mistake in opening up to them about this. I still don't know whether I was right in tearing down so many boundaries between us. All I know is I wanted to be authentic with them and to tell them what was going on in my life. And I wanted to know what was going on in their lives.

They quizzed me constantly about my sons and my wife. "Yo, Jay. You fuck other women?"

"No."

"Come on, Jay. Tell us the truth."

"I'm serious. I don't mess around."

"Why not?"

"There are a lot of reasons, but the main one is that it would hurt my wife. I don't want her messing around on me, so why would I mess around on her?"

"But you don't gotta tell her."

"No, but if I did it and I didn't tell her, *I'd* know and then I'd despise myself. I couldn't live like that. I'd go crazy, you know? I'd self-destruct. There's something in me that if I mess up, I end up punishing myself by messing up more."

"But what if your wife be playin' you with some other nigga?"

"That's her problem. I promised her I wouldn't do that and she promised me she wouldn't, and I hope she's keeping her end of the bargain. But, you're right. I don't know what's going on with her. I'm pretty sure things are cool. I have no reason to assume they're not. But you know, I really don't know when push comes to shove."

"What if you go home and she be fucking some other nigga? What you gonna do?"

"I don't know."

"Would you shoot his ass?"

"I don't know. But I don't think I'd be as pissed at the guy as I would be at her."

"What 'chu mean?"

"Well, you know, even if he were my best friend, it's not as if he made some vow to me that he wouldn't sleep with my wife, right? But my wife, you know, she did make a vow to me. So I'd feel much more pissed at her than at him."

"So what you would do to her?"

"I'd probably say, 'See ya.' I wouldn't do anything to her. At least I hope I wouldn't."

"Man, if I found my woman fucking around, I'd put a cap in her ass and I'd put a cap in his ass too."

"But what good would that do you? How would it change anything? You'd still feel hurt about what happened, right? And you'd just get arrested. I mean the cops come and find the bodies of your wife and another man in your apartment? It doesn't take a brain surgeon to know what happened."

"No, but I won't be shooting them then. I wait and when I see him on the street, I'm shootin' his ass, make it look like somebody stuck him up. Same for my wife."

"But how would that make you feel any better?"

"Cause then I know they don't be doin' that shit again."

"Wouldn't it be easier just to get a divorce?"

"But she got to learn that she can't mess with me."

"How's she going to learn if she's dead?"

"Well, my next wife will know it."

"So what if you had kids. You'd just shoot their mother?"

It would often go like that when we'd speak about it from a moral or ethical angle. We'd talk about how a person should live his life. There would be three or four kids answering my questions and asking me questions and raising possibilities and everyone else would be listening.

They liked talking about hypothetical questions like that and I sometimes felt like they were not arguing with me as much as they were trying to think about it from a number of perspectives. And, of course, a discussion of that sort was preferable to doing school work. And though I knew that, I believed, and still do, that conversations of that sort had their place out there.

Moments like these made teaching out there feel meaningful, but I could never find a formula that would allow me to create those moments. If they didn't arise on their own, they felt forced. There came a point when I made peace with that fact.

This was true not only for conversations of that sort. It was true for teaching in general. Finding a formula was as impossible as coming up with a unified field theory. I stopped looking for it. I continued to plan, but I did so with the attitude of a man in a sailboat rather than in a motorized boat. I planned knowing that I was at the mercy of the winds and the currents. I knew where I wanted to go, but I also knew that getting there without a lot of twists and turns would be impossible. Maintaining control of the classroom could only occur by relinquishing some of that control to my students.

After I accepted that fact, teaching began to seem nearly effortless. For one thing, I didn't worry as much. And other than planning, it wasn't as if grading my students' work took all that long. Most days I was able to get my grading done during my prep period.

The kids were writing, but if I had a class of fifteen, it was rare that I'd get more than a couple pieces of writing over a page long. When a GED examination was a couple of weeks away, all of the Sprungs teachers would focus on helping prepare them.

I would borrow the large screen television and a computer from Mr. Cumberbatch in the computer room and we would write an essay together. A successful GED essay included an introductory paragraph, two body paragraphs and a conclusion. There were several of us who pushed for the five paragraph essay—three body paragraphs—but four paragraphs was the way it had always been taught on Rikers. In the past we'd had a high percentage of students pass with four paragraphs, so we agreed that the simpler we kept it the better.

I would find a question that had been asked on a previous exam and the students and I would discuss the question together, figure out how to break it down, develop a thesis statement and a couple of reasons to support that thesis. After that, we'd develop examples to support the reasons. Kids' writing improved significantly during those two weeks. History, Science, and Math teachers were also prepping our students so that many of them passed the GED. The rest of the time I'd focus on having them write personal narrative essays or having them read short essays.

After I had been teaching there for four or five months, there were very few students left who remembered when I had not known what I was doing. New kids would come in, see the other kids doing my work and they'd follow along. It seemed magical.

In order to get certified, I had to do a student teaching equivalency. A woman came in from the Board of Ed for those of us in that situation and once a week she would meet with me to talk about the way things were going. She made sure I knew how to do lesson plans that had clear objectives and that I knew how to execute them. She would also observe me teaching once a week and talk to me about the way the class had gone. After a few weeks of this, she gave me a certificate that was equivalent to having completed student teaching.

11. Points of View

By the end of my first school year, there had been a significant turnover among the faculty. It was difficult to predict who was going to stay. It was also difficult to determine whether people left on their own, or whether The Ladies had shown them the door.

When I came back the second year, even Mr. Rhodes was no longer with us, nor was Mr. Aceves. I never found out where they went or why they left, but I couldn't imagine that The Ladies didn't have a hand in it. The year after I left, I'm told Mr. Rhodes returned. He and I were never close, but I always appreciated the way he looked out for Sprung teachers.

One of the new people who came was Bill. He had an MA in physics from the University of Chicago and he had nearly completed his PhD at Columbia. The thought of having him teach science to kids who since first grade had rarely attended school seemed like overkill. The thing was, even when he encountered kids who showed no interest in science, he'd hook them by explaining obscure details of physics in a way that would blow their minds. And then he'd teach them more basic scientific concepts.

Another teacher who began out there was Paul. He had taught in a number of places, but when I first met him he struck me as a bit naive for a place like Rikers. By the time I left, I felt Rikers was a bit naive for a guy like Paul. He was very smart and he got a lot out of the kids. He went on to become a successful writer of young adult fiction. Many of the themes of his novels concerned situations similar to those our students faced not only on Rikers, but on the streets where they lived.

Mr. Stryker, an art teacher, came at about that time. When I first met him, he seemed very different from my later impression of him. In the beginning, he would hang out over at the administrative trailer between classes, just standing there as if he didn't know what to do with himself. I remember talking to him and having the impression that I was dealing with a really shy guy. I guess the reality is that he was just trying to get to know the lay of the land. He got it soon enough.

After he had been there a couple months, we had an assembly and Mr. Stryker went up front with the microphone and you could not shut him up. He was up there dancing and rapping about how he was Mr. Stryker and he taught on Rikers and he was a very funny guy. The kids loved him. He became a minor celebrity on our part of the island.

There had been a television show called *In Living Color* on which Damon Wayans played a character by the name of Homey the Clown. Homey was Black and tough and he thought he was very powerful, but in the end he was just a clown. He had a bald head with tufts of hair sticking out either side.

One day during lunch, Ms. Jaynes showed up with a man who definitely resembled Homey. She said to me, "Mr. Trash, I'd like you to meet Mr. Maybury. He's going to be teaching math, and he needs to be shown around. He'll follow you around for the rest of the day, if that's all right with you."

Mr. Maybury and I talked for a few minutes in the teachers' room. Soon I heard the kids stomping as they entered the trailer. Maybury was a very formal Black man who dressed the part, but from the shoulders up, he was a glasses-wearing version of Homey the Clown. I wondered how he would do with these kids. I could never predict their response to a new teacher, but I was pretty sure they'd be calling him Homey.

We walked down to my room and as soon as the two of us walked in front of the window, I heard the first kid yell to the others, "Look, it's Homey." As we entered the room, every single kid in there was yelling, "Hey, Homey," and "Yo, it's Homey, the motherfucking clown."

Now if Maybury had been slightly less formal and less brittle—in short, if he'd been a completely different person—he would have had some sort of comeback. But you could see Maybury standing there and recreating the world even as it flowed toward him. He was creating a world in which the kids were not calling him Homey the Clown. There was no way anyone would call him a clown. I'd be surprised if he even knew who Homey was.

Walking into a room under such circumstances was a tough thing for anyone. Being made fun of is not something most people seek out. And it wasn't as if I could make these kids stop. No one had control over them which is why they were in jail. They didn't mind looking someone in the eye and sticking them up and taking their money or their watches and chains and in some cases shooting them. So when it came to insulting a person, it was child's play for them. It didn't matter that Mr. Maybury was right there in front of them and it didn't matter that he had feelings just like anyone else. And it didn't matter that he was entering a completely new situation. Empathy played no role, at least not when they were together. They all looked him right in the eye as if he were a piece of cake, and they ate him up. Or they tried to. I wasn't sure how Mr. Maybury was handling it. The fact that he was so formal worried me.

I shouted above them, "Yo... Yo. Listen up. Yo. Okay, now this is Mr. Maybury. He's going to be teaching math out here and I want you all to show him some respect. He's going to sit down and observe for now, but in a few days he'll be teaching you. So I want you all to just chill."

One of the kids raised his hand, which was rare, so I should have known something was up. I called on him.

"Yo, Jay, say word to mother he don't look just like Homey the Clown."

I said, "What's wrong with you? Are you trying to make fun of someone you don't even know? He's in a new situation and you need to make him feel welcome. You want to make fun of someone, make fun of me, all right?"

Another kid raised his hand. I called on him.

"Yo, Jay. You ugly."

"Thank you. Anyone else."

"You's a dumb mother fucker, Jay."

"Thank you. Anyone else."

"Jay, you White."

I said, "Damn, you sure know how to hurt a guy."

They all laughed and I noticed that Mr. Maybury was sitting there looking confused. After I got to know him, it seemed to me that he didn't pick up everything that came his way. It was not that he was unintelligent, though it sometimes appeared that way. My take on him is that he pondered things in chunks. Something would happen and he'd sit there digesting it, mulling it over. Meanwhile, other things were happening, but he was too busy processing the first event and was not picking up these new events. He would come to, observe the new moment, but since he'd missed the intervening moments, the new event was out of context so it made no sense. So he'd ponder that, trying to solve its mystery, thereby missing the next moment. This is how he appeared to live his life, which is not the ideal frame of mind for a place like Rikers.

But after a few weeks, he somehow did all right out there, mostly, I think, because he was such a nice guy and completely genuine.

One day I was talking to him and Dr. Steele in the hallway when a passing student came over and shook hands with me and started talking to me. We exchanged a few words and then the kid went on his way. Mr. Maybury then asked me, "Mr. Trask. There is something I have been meaning to ask you. Are you a Black man?"

I said, "What?"

I'd heard him, but I needed to replay it to see if he was being sarcastic or making fun of me or what. I couldn't imagine that he actually thought I was Black.

"Are you a Black man?"

I was also trying to figure out how to answer him in a way that let him know I didn't mind being mistaken for a Black man—Malcolm X was definitely right in pointing out that nearly all White people wish they were Black, which is why he said we go out and sit in the sun to darken our skin.

I said, "No, not that I'm aware of."

He said, "You have a way with these kids that I can't explain except by thinking that you must be Black and it just doesn't show."

I thanked him. I was embarrassed that Dr. Steele was present for the exchange. I was certain that he, being more sophisticated than Mr. Maybury, saw me as White through and through. Which, by the way, is not to say anything against Dr. Steele. I admired the man deeply. He had been around the block enough times to know what was what and who was who. I think all of us out there felt like he could see through us. The thing that gave him his power was he never told you what your issues were. But it seemed clear that he saw them. It's great to have a man like him around. It helps to awaken you just a bit.

There was also a counselor out there named Maybury. He was a tall, thin Black man who was completely bald—no eyelashes or brows, no hair anywhere on his body. I heard him tell the students that he had alopecia. He would show up from time to time and make the rounds to different classes and talk to the kids. One day he came to my classroom. Normally teachers left when he came in, because it gave them an extra prep, but I asked if I could sit in. He gave me his blessing.

He told the kids about how he had been a criminal. His crime of choice was burglary. I remember him saying that whenever he did a crime, he tried to set it up so that he wouldn't get more than ten years if he were caught. "I was prepared to do a dime," he said. "But I was not prepared to do two of them." For that reason, and because he had no desire to be violent, he never brought a gun or knife to the job.

The kids were all silent as he told his story about getting arrested and being hit with a twenty year sentence. He was sent to prison and while he was there he decided to change his life and stop hanging out with negative people. He went through college in prison, majoring in psychology. Eventually, while still a prisoner himself, he began working with incarcerated men who were interested in changing. They let him out early. After earning his MA in counseling and a lot of persistence, he had been able to get this job talking to inmates on Rikers.

He told the kids that though they might be judged to be felons, they shouldn't give up the idea of eventually landing successful jobs. He told of doctors, lawyers, clergymen he knew, all of whom had done hard time. He gave the kids a lot of hope that they could turn their lives around.

Mr. Locke was another teacher whom I got to know. He was a tall Black man from one of the Caribbean Islands who taught in the second trailer. Locke had actually been there longer than I had, but because he was in the other trailer, I rarely interacted with him. He was an intelligent man who made a point of not being taken for a fool. As a result, he sometimes felt slighted by other teachers, which led to arguments.

I remember one day hearing someone yelling. It sounded like an actual fight might break out. I looked out my window into the hallway and there stood Mr. Locke gesticulating and yelling. Mr. Scott kept trying to explain that he hadn't meant it like that—I never did find out what "it" was. In the end, Scott was yelling too and they entertained the rest of us for several minutes. Later, a similar thing happened between Locke and me.

We were sitting at the same table in the cafeteria and we began discussing the role of women in society. His view was more traditional than mine, and we were both insistent that the other be quiet and listen. At some point I realized that the two of us were yelling at each other and everyone was watching us. We finally left and a couple days later we saw each other in the hall and grinned and shook hands. From that point on, we were friends.

There were lots of arguments out there among teachers. Many of these arguments were between Mr. Salek and several White teachers about whether the White man's version of history could be trusted. Salek was a very good sport about it, but some of the White teachers grumbled about how they couldn't believe he was teaching such crazy stuff to the kids when everyone knew that he was contradicting centuries of historical fact. Salek would calmly ask them if they had ever heard of historical "facts" that turned out to be inaccurate and they'd say he was being ridiculous.

Salek had about the most amazingly deep and melodious voice I've ever heard. I never saw him get flustered. He was confident regardless of the situation he was in. Though he taught a version of history that often didn't concur with the White man's version, he knew both versions intimately.

According to him, from the time of the Pre-Socratics up through Aristotle's day, many Greek philosophers and thinkers spent time in Africa from where they appropriated a number of important ideas and theorems; moreover, he claimed that many of the great advances in Greek culture were the result of those ideas. He said this was true in the worlds of mathematics, architecture, engineering, philosophy, medicine, horticulture as well as government. He claimed, in fact, that Pythagoras' ideas, including his eponymous theorem, were in existence in Africa before Pythagoras was born.

He would teach this view of history to the kids but he would also teach them the standard view. He might then point out an inconsistency within that view. I admired him. I've always felt that by teaching history as he did, that is, by showing the way the "White view" of history differs from the "Black view," he was actually teaching kids to be critical of what they heard and read. As far as I'm concerned, that is one of the integral parts of a sound education.

Bill and I argued about one idea in particular fairly regularly. He was an expert in statistics because of all the work he'd done with quantum mechanics in graduate school. Though I know nothing about math, I had a pet belief about statistics.

"So," I'd say. "It's accepted, is it not, that statistics would only be completely reliable with respect, say, to rolling a ten-sided die, if you were to roll the die an infinite number of times, right? And if I'm not mistaken, it's also accepted that the smaller the number of rolls of the die, the less reliable statistics becomes, right? Okay, so say you were rolling our ten-sided die a trillion times. In all likelihood, each side would come up roughly ten percent of the time, right? But if you were rolling it only a hundred times, it could happen that a particular side would come up fifty percent of the time, another side thirty percent, and the other twenty percent might be split among seven of the remaining eight sides; one of the sides might not even come up at all. Right?

"If you follow that thinking to its logical end, each time you reduce the number of rolls, the less accurate the statistical outcome will be, until when it gets down to rolling the die only one time, statistics are completely unreliable. At that point, if you're betting on a particular side coming up, either you'll win or you'll lose, that is, it's a fifty-fifty proposition."

This would drive Bill nuts. He knew all sorts of mathematical and statistical terms and distinctions about which I knew nothing, but I was unwilling to give up my theory. One day after our students had left, half of the Sprungs staff was gathered around us as Bill and I argued about this and they were laughing their heads off as I insisted that it was a fifty-fifty proposition.

Bill played it up big. He said, "So you admit that you know nothing about math. And you admit further that you know nothing about statistics. You know nothing about anything, and yet you're arguing with me about this and you have no basis from which to argue."

I said, "Don't give me that bullshit. You're trying to win the argument based on authority. The Middle Ages are over."

All the other teachers were laughing and of course, they were on Bill's side, but a couple of weeks later, I'd try my argument again.

I don't know why it was, but argumentation at RIEF among teachers was more natural than any place I've ever taught.

And, yes, I know . . . . Bill was right.

Probably.

12. Scratch a Skeptic

Class was just finishing one day and I was reading something a student had handed me from his lawyer. As I tried to make sense of it for him, a kid walked up behind me and pretended to put me in what the kids all called a "sleeper hold."

A sleeper hold involves locking one's arms around the sides of a person's neck so as to block the flow of blood through the carotid arteries. After a few seconds, if applied correctly, the victim goes unconscious. But this kid was just playing around and not squeezing hard at all. Absentmindedly, I stuck my arm back over my shoulder, grabbed him under his arm pit and yanked. I wasn't even trying to flip him, but the next thing I knew the kid had flown over my shoulder and was sitting unharmed at my feet on the floor. I was as surprised as he was. The kids who saw it were saying, "Did you see that?" and "Oh, shit," and "Jay be knowin' some moves."

They all asked me what martial art I knew. Was it karate, judo, or what? Someone thought it might be jujitsu. At first I protested and said I didn't know anything. They were all like, "Shit, he must know it good, 'cause he don't even be braggin' about it." The more I protested, the more convinced they became that I had some sort of black belt.

It got to the point where if a new kid came in who was giving me shit, the other kids would warn him, "Don't be messin' with Jay. He know that Chinese shit."

White man that I am, I began to take advantage of it. When someone gave me shit, I would kick off my shoes, place my hands together, and bow. Everyone would move back as if they expected me to tear the kid apart right there in front of them. Sometimes I was amazed at how gullible the students were. During those moments, the skepticism they normally displayed seemed like a front to hide their gullibility. Scratch a skeptic and you get a believer.

This is not to say they were gullible in every respect. For instance, they didn't believe the news and they didn't believe anyone's promises to them that something good might happen in the future. But when it came to stories about strength, evil, or any kind of bad news they were all over it.

There was that story I mentioned about the White captain who had a tattoo of a White baby holding a rope from which was hanging a dead Black baby and underneath it supposedly said, "KKK." I kept hearing that story from kids. Finally I began asking teachers who had been on the island for a while. Both White and Black teachers claimed it was a story that had been circulating since they'd been there. You would never find a kid who had seen this tattoo, but they believed it anyway. The story made sense to them because that was the way they imagined White people to be.

It parallels exactly the way a huge percentage of White people in this country who have never actually known an African American, an Hispanic, or an Arab, believe what they're told about those groups by television, movies, the news, and our President.

A lot of the Black kids on the island had never actually had dealings with White people. Many lived in Black neighborhoods out of which they rarely traveled. Many had attended schools where the principal and teachers were Black or Hispanic, and they lived in neighborhoods where the store owners were as well. After they got to know me, a few kids told me I was the first White person they'd actually gotten to know.

There was this kid in one of my classes who used to leave every time I entered the classroom. One day I was standing outside the door waiting for the other teacher to leave before I went in. The kid saw me through the window and he walked out the door as I entered. I said to him, "What is it with you? Every time I come in here you have a look on your face like you've just seen a White man." He laughed and that day he stayed and we became fairly good friends.

*　　*　　*

When I first got to the Sprungs Carlos had already been an inmate there for a couple of months. He stayed there for over a year after I arrived. The thing is, Rikers is a jail, not a prison. You're supposed to stay there while you are awaiting your trial, and that's it. Right to a speedy trial? If you're lucky.

Now, it did happen that inmates who had been tried and sentenced to a year or less remained on Rikers. The thing is, they were sent to a different part of the island. Inmates in the Sprungs and in the part of the building serviced by RIEF were all awaiting trial. I never did learn what the holdup was on Carlos' case, but it always struck me as odd. And by the way, this was true for several other students of mine as well, including Tony.

Carlos had witnessed my second lesson out there, the second "fuck" lesson I'd bombed so badly. He had joined in with the other kids when they were laughing at me. At that point, he had seemed incorrigible to me. Later, when he was moved into another classroom, I got to know him and he seemed like such an innocent. It was often like that out there, even more than on the outside. You'd meet a kid, think he was destined for hell, and then you'd get to know him and he'd be transformed. When that happened, I always wondered, "Did he change or did I?"

Carlos was incredibly patient about the time he was spending there. He never let it get to him. In fact, I think he somehow liked being there. He accrued a kind of power over time with the COs, with the school, and with the kids.

On a number of occasions he was helpful to me. There were times when I had to substitute during my prep period in the class of non-English speaking Hispanic kids. Carlos would come in with me and translate.

Going in there with Carlos had been one thing. I'd say something in English and Carlos would translate for me. The kids all liked Carlos, and because he was getting along well with me, they liked me by default. But after Carlos left, I was on my own. I remember the first time I went in there without him. By that time I knew a couple of kids in there, but most of them had arrived since the last time I had "taught" them. I went in and said, "Will you guys teach me Spanish?"

"Si, we Spanish."

"You teach me? You teach me Spanish?"

"Si. I Spanish."

"Right, but you teach me Spanish?"

"You want the Spanish?"

My plan was that in teaching me Spanish, they would also learn a bit of English.

They spoke among themselves and soon they were all laughing and teaching me words. They were exceptionally polite, the politest class of students I had out there. Because of the way I behaved when I was a kid, I tended to believe they were teaching me swears and making believe they were very polite words. When I checked with other Spanish speakers, however, I found they were being truthful. In fact, most of them seemed so innocent, I couldn't imagine them doing anything to hurt anyone.

One day, at the behest of his classmates, one of them lifted his shirt and showed me an amazing number of bullet holes in his torso. I don't remember the exact number, but there were so many I couldn't believe he survived.

He and a friend tried to explain it to me, but I couldn't make sense of what they were saying. One of them ran across the hall and got an English speaking Hispanic kid who went by the name Machete. He came in and translated.

He explained to me that the kid had been selling drugs on someone else's corner and though he'd been warned not to sell there, he kept on. Finally, a car drove past and in a classic drive-by, several people shot him and left him for dead. He still had some of the bullets in his body and I swear his breath had a potent metallic smell that I've never encountered before.

I was surprised at how gentle Machete seemed when he was with his Spanish speaking friends. Ordinarily he was such a tough guy. He had such a chip on his shoulder.

Several months before that, he came into my room one day while I was teaching and stood up by the board next to me, pretending to be teaching the class. He kept imitating me and he wouldn't shut up and he wouldn't leave. At first we all thought it was funny, but after a few minutes of this, I began to want it to end. Especially when he began telling everyone that I was his woman.

I stood there grinning for a few seconds, and then I grabbed him, picked him up and knocked his legs out from under him and laid him gently on the floor. All the kids in the room applauded. They all asked him why he let his woman treat him like that. I helped him to his feet and he left the room with a red face.

I didn't know it at the time, but that moment was observed by a CO who told the dep on me. More about that later.

Another time Machete was sitting at a desk and would not be quiet. I went over to him and put my hand on his desk and told him he had a choice. If he wanted to stay in the room, he had to be quiet. If he didn't, I was going to send him out and he could take his chances with the COs.

He was holding a freshly sharpened pencil in his hand that he held like a knife above my hand. He said to me, "No, you got a choice. If you want to keep your hand, take it off my desk."

A kid's desk was his territory and kids didn't want you to touch it if there was the slightest friction between you. He was grinning and I knew he wasn't actually angry. He just had to keep up his image as undefeatable even though it was an image he'd never managed to hang onto for more than a few minutes at a time.

I kept my hand there to make a point and I just looked at him so he'd see

I was serious. He began lowering his hand—the one holding the pencil—as if he intended to stab my hand, but he did so in slow motion. The whole time he's looking me in the eye and grinning.

I feel the pencil point contact my hand. I can feel that it's sharp and it stings a little, but not enough to qualify as pain. He does this again and again and we just keep looking each other in the eye, and he keeps grinning. Everyone else in the class is looking at us and laughing because we are, after all, a couple of clowns. Everyone knows that on some level we're cut from the same cloth.

Machete keeps bringing his hand up and lowering it. After a minute or so, he looks down and his grin changes to a look of alarm. He says, "Oh, shit," and he looks scared. Now I look down and see maybe ten tiny points of blood on my hand where the point of the pencil has punctured the skin ever so slightly.

Everyone else is gathering around us now and they're all saying "Oh shit," and the like, and they all expect Machete is going to get his ass fried because I'm obviously going to tell on him. I found a napkin and wiped it off and said to him, "So Machete, I don't want to hear any more shit from you." I continued teaching and he shut up after that and never gave me any more trouble.

I didn't think any more about it until the next day. When I entered my homeroom I practically received a hero's welcome. The incident with Machete had happened in a completely different classroom and I was all confused about what they were talking about.

One of the kids said to me, "Yo, Jay. Show us where Machete stabbed you." It turned out that they all thought I was incredible because I didn't "snitch" on Machete. I told them there was nothing to tell, that it had barely broken the skin, that it wasn't as if I had actually been stabbed or even hurt. I showed them my hand. By now there was nothing to see except a few little pinpoint scabs. But the students had such a need to believe in something that reality didn't matter.

Machete was a hero because he'd "stabbed" a teacher and gotten away with it.

I was a hero because I had been stabbed by an inmate and hadn't snitched.

13. Twofold Nature

The school provided absolutely no budget to English teachers. History, math, science, and law teachers all had textbooks, but it appeared that no such thing was available to English teachers. If I had persisted, I'm sure I could have gotten something. The fact is, I have never seen an English textbook I liked, and I couldn't imagine one that would do anything for these kids.

I began to consider having the students read *The Autobiography of Malcolm X*. A lot of them spoke about Malcolm, but when I asked them questions, they didn't seem to know anything about him. I wasn't sure how I was going to use the book. In each of the classrooms, there was a steady turnover of students.

I finally decided to make copies of the book, one chapter at a time. I'd go into a classroom and hand out the copies and together we'd read the chapter. I would read aloud for ten minutes or so to get them into the chapter, and then I'd ask individual kids to read a paragraph.

Some of them read really well, which amazed me because so many of them had spent very little time in school. Even in the lower grades, their lives in many cases had been so haphazard that school was what they did when their mothers had the wherewithal to check on them. While it's true that a significant percentage of their mothers were addicts of one sort or another, many of their mothers were single parents who struggled just to make ends meet by working a couple of minimum wage jobs.

After that, we would discuss what we had read and liken it to situations they'd been in. Then the next day, I'd ask them to review what had happened in the story so far, not only for kids who had missed the previous day, but also for kids who had been there. Once every few days I'd have them write something about the book. Sometimes I'd have them answer a series of factual questions about Malcolm's life. Other times I'd have them put themselves into a situation that Malcolm found himself in and write about it, those sorts of things. But I never did this with blank pages. I continued to write a question at the top of the page with lines for them to write their answers on. We moved slowly through the book and every day the kids looked forward to hearing the next installment.

There was one class in particular who appreciated the Malcolm X readings. It was my second birthday out there, and they gave me one of my favorite presents I have ever received.

There were only about eight or nine kids in that room and they were all fairly good friends. I told them it was my birthday and suddenly one of them went into this completely spontaneous rap about how much I was doing for the kids on Rikers. I would do anything to have a recording or a transcript of it. I was completely amazed not only by the quality of the rhythm, rhyme, and flow, but also by the feeling he put into it.

When he had gone on for a minute or so, he tapped the kid beside him and said "Pass it on, pass it on, pass it on," and then that kid began rhyming about me as well. And when he finished, he too tapped the next kid in line and this time all of them said in unison, "Pass it on, pass it on, pass it on."

They went on like this, right across the classroom until every kid had had a chance to rap. If each of the students had written his part in advance, I would have been impressed. But the fact that they free-styled this blew me away. It was the first time I had a clear understanding of how talented my students were. And how generous. I could not get over the amount of appreciation they showed.

It was the moment that provided my greatest feeling of fulfillment on the island. And simultaneously, it left me with a feeling of despair at what a waste it was to have this talent walled off from the rest of society.

*   *   *

School Based Management (SBM) is a system whereby the teachers and administration, and to a degree, the students, run a school collectively. When it works, they jointly come up with goals and develop plans for achieving those goals. The result is supposed to be that everyone begins to take more of an interest in the affairs of the school rather than feeling that decisions come at them from on high.

By the middle of my second school year, SBM meetings were taking place two mornings a week before school began. We'd get there and spend an hour in meetings. Sometimes we'd meet with our departments and sometimes we'd meet with people working on a particular grant writing project. It always seemed to me that the people on the inner circle of SBM had trouble coming up with things for us to do. We'd often sit in rooms with small groups of people and talk. I began calling SBM, "Slow Bowel Movement."

It was during one of those morning meetings that a new teacher by the name of Rumi appeared. I took an immediate liking to him. Not long after we met, he showed me some of his poetry which was powerful and had an intensity I had not seen in him during our conversations. Up until then, I had thought of him as mellow and laid back. Soon enough I came to realize that while he did have that mellow side, there was more to him than that.

Many faculty members began referring to him as Malcolm—some lovingly, some not so. He often spoke about the injustices endured by the Black man at the hands of the White man and how corrupt the system was that the White man had built.

Over time, he and I became the best of friends. We taught the same students, even though we were both English teachers. RIEF sometimes had difficulty finding a full complement of teachers to cover the various subject areas, so it sometimes happened that a particular group of kids got two teachers from the same subject area.

At about the same time Rumi started, we acquired a student named Angelo. I first met him one Monday morning. I walked into my homeroom and there he was. He had arrived on Saturday, I believe, and by the time Monday morning rolled around, he was in charge. Not in a way that the other kids would have acknowledged. He managed to be in charge without anyone suspecting it. He didn't seem to threaten anyone.

Angelo was well named. He really looked and sometimes acted like an Angel. He was a beautiful kid. He was small, Hispanic, intelligent. Intelligence was a fairly common attribute on Rikers. It was a quality that you couldn't help but notice. The thing to remember is that most of the kids out there had been businessmen, entrepreneurs since their early teens; moreover, many of them had been living by their wits since learning to walk. For some of them, their day to day lives had been a matter of life and death since birth. For most kids, fun and games begin in the afternoon after school lets out, but for many of our students, it was school that was fun and games. After school, that's when life got serious. This was true for them on the island and off it.

That first day Angelo was there, we were reading *The Autobiography of Malcolm X*. I began the reading and when I asked if anyone else wanted to read, Angelo raised his hand. Not only was he able to decode all of the words that he came upon: he was able to read them with the appropriate tone and voice and feeling. He read aloud better than most college graduates. It felt to me that everyone was blown away by his reading—I know I was.

When we spoke about what we had read, Angelo dominated the conversation. He had all sorts of ideas about Malcolm's experiences and he had his own unique view about what they meant. He provided all sorts of examples from his own life to back up his ideas. All of the other kids sat back and listened to the conversation Angelo and I were having.

He said he wanted to be like Malcolm X. I wondered how the Black kids in the class would react to an Hispanic kid claiming their Malcolm as his own. But they had no trouble with it. Malcolm was big enough to go around.

The next day things proceeded similarly. As soon as I entered the room, he rushed up and wanted to help pass out the photocopies of the passage we were reading so we could get as much reading time in as possible. Again he read aloud and again he dominated the conversation. He was a force. He was far smaller than anyone else in the class. He was thin and short. He had hardly enough flesh for muscle, but it was clear that no one was going to mess with this kid. He'd had on nice clothes his first day. Today he still had them on. That was rare for a little guy.

I suppose the argument could be made that no one else was small enough to fit his clothes, but if you'd been there you'd have seen something else was going on.

After I got to know him a bit, Angelo would sometimes pout. He became a peevish elementary school child during those times. But no one made fun of him the way they would have made fun of anyone else who behaved that way. I actually don't think they were afraid of him, but I may be wrong. I'd sooner think it's that he was so much himself that everyone admired him for it. I think they also admired Angelo's intelligence. Whatever the reason, he could sit there and complain and whine about how bad things were and no one would say shit to him. They'd just sit and listen.

Of course there's also the possibility that he was under the protection of one of the tougher kids in the Sprungs. In that case no one would have been willing to mess with him either. I don't really know. All I know is that when he complained and pouted, no one called him on it. When this took up class time, I'd say, "Come on, Angelo. Let's get back to Malcolm," and he would get completely pissed at me.

Sometimes he'd tell me he was never going to speak to me again. But he'd always get over it within a few hours. Sometimes when I'd leave the class, he wouldn't be speaking to me. Later in the day he'd come by the room I was in and apologize and say that tomorrow he wanted to be the first one to read. I'd say, "Okay, Angelo."

I really liked him. He was in there for selling drugs. One day he told me he was fourteen when he began bringing home money for the family. Angelo said his father, who was unemployed, didn't like the idea. His mother didn't like it either, but she tended to look the other way so they could pay the rent and put food on the table. That's all he told me about the situation, but it was a window into these kids' lives that I hadn't considered before.

I spent a lot of time peeping through that window, and what I witnessed fired my imagination. What would it be like to live under those conditions? I'd picture myself as an unemployed father, lacking the means to make money. I walk into the kitchen and there's my son handing my wife a wad of bills. Of course I would hate having my son selling drugs. But I would also hate having him usurp my role as breadwinner. Here I am in the prime of my life, and there's my son, a snot-nosed fourteen year old, and what's he doing? He's bringing home the bacon. The order would be screwed up. The first would be last; the last would be first. To me it just didn't seem like a good idea.

*   *   *

Rumi got along famously with Angelo. Rumi had a gift for getting our students involved in discussions about topics that matter—race, spirituality, what it means to be a man, what it means to be a Black man in this society. Angelo was completely enthralled with those discussions. Rumi and I had hopes for Angelo but we also had worries. Angelo knew we were his champions, and he had other teachers who encouraged him as well, especially Bill.

The thing that worried me most about Angelo was his radically twofold nature. When he talked during class, he sounded like he was all about changing his life and getting an education. But several times I entered the room and found him talking like a total gangster. His tone during those moments was completely unrepentant as he bragged about crimes he'd committed. He seemed like a completely different kid in those moments. The argument could be made that he was being sincere when he spoke to us and that the other side, the gangster side, was a mask to keep his fellow inmates from messing with him. And if those other kids were to hear him speak all day as though he were simply a seeker of knowledge, they would think he was a herb.

The other possibility and the one I believe more likely is that both sides that he expressed were genuine.

I had that same experience with other students as well. At the same time Angelo was there, in the next room over—the room that had rapped to me on my birthday—there was a Black student who was exceptionally quiet. Slowly, after he got to know me, he began to take part in the class. He had a wandering eye that gave him a comical appeal. He was always complaining in an Eeyore sort of way. And then when you'd call him on it, he'd always say, "I'm sayin' though," but he'd say it out of the side of his mouth and "sayin'" would come out as "shayin" and the "sh" would whistle. I tended to view him as a harmless kid who'd basically made a couple of bad choices.

One day after the turtles had woken them the previous night, I recognized that nothing was going to happen that day, so I sat around with them and we all told stories about things we regretted, things that I hoped I could eventually get them to write about. I told the first story about a friend of mine, Rene, who had committed suicide. Back when I was living on West 122nd Street, he called me at about 2:00 a.m. He was laughing hysterically. I said, "What's up, Rene?"

He said, "I tried to kill myself by taking a bottle of sleeping pills. But all that happened is I woke up with a headache. I'm such a failure I can't even kill myself properly. So I called you hoping you'd have a better idea for how to get the job done." Once again he went into nonstop laughter.

I was still half asleep and as I tried to figure out how to respond, I was quiet.

After a few seconds of this he said, "It's okay, Jason. Don't be shocked."

"I'm not shocked," I said. "I'm just trying to think of a better way."

We both laughed and I suggested that we meet down at the College Inn, an all-night Greek restaurant on Broadway between 111th and 112th.

We met there a few minutes later and talked about everything that had been going on in Rene's life. He'd had one too many short stories rejected and he felt there was no hope he would ever be published.

I stayed there with him for several hours telling him he had to just keep at it, just keep writing, and I reminded him of Woody Allen's line about showing up. By the time we left, he promised me he wouldn't do it, and he seemed genuinely upbeat.

A week or so later, I left New York City for Maine, where I spent the summer. When I returned in late August, I learned that Rene had jumped in front of a subway and was dead. I felt terrible about it, not only because I'd lost a good friend, but because of the cavalier way I'd responded to him.

The students asked me a few questions, and then someone else told a story. I sat back and listened, trying to disappear so their stories would be unaffected by my presence. Apparently I succeeded.

Eeyore told a story about riding in a taxi. He claimed he'd been sitting behind the driver and he pulled a gun on the guy and told him to give him his money.

Hoping to make Eeyore afraid to shoot, the man began driving really fast. Eeyore was quite scared, and when they drove over a pothole, his gun when off and shot the man in the back of the head.

Eeyore began laughing as he told us this last part of the story. It was an odd laugh. It didn't sound as if he thought his experience funny. It had a quality of helplessness to it.

He described how the bullet had gone through the guy's head and out through the windshield. He said blood and brain splattered all over the place. He was the only one laughing. No one joined him. We all sat there in an awkward silence. It took him a few seconds to catch on. He looked around, confused. In that moment, I believe he had a realization of what he had done.

Or maybe he didn't. The thing is, you could never tell. For all I know, he may have made the entire thing up.

14. Scratch a Carrot

Until maybe a century ago, few people cared about what went on inside prisons and jails. As a result, they were hard, cold places completely lacking in the sorts of comforts and niceties that would make the lives of its inhabitants tolerable. Many inmates had to sleep on hard surfaces without actual mattresses and they were miserable.

During my time as a teacher on Rikers, I sometimes wondered if modern attempts to make houses of detention more habitable may have actually had the opposite effect. Phones, for instance. On the face of it, allowing inmates the opportunity to call home on a daily basis sounds like an enlightened idea. But in a jail, the more enlightened an idea, the more degrading it becomes in practice.

As long as our students were not in trouble with their COs, they were allowed one 6-minute phone call every day. In theory.

The problem is, in a correctional facility, privileges of that sort quickly devolve into coercive devices. Scratch a carrot and you have a stick.

My impression is that few COs manage privileges of this sort: a few, because they are lazy and feel that keeping track of such details is beneath them; others, because allowing the toughest inmates a modicum of control gives the COs a handle on them. And it is also true that a small minority of COs get off on watching brutality unfold.

I saw the inside of the Sprung that housed the cafeteria a number of times, but I saw the inside of a Sprungs barracks on only one occasion. I went in there at the end of the school day to bring a photocopy of the passage we had read from *The Autobiography of Malcolm X* to a student who had missed class because he'd been in court. I had been looking for an excuse to go in there and now I had one.

I spoke to the two on-duty officers who were sitting in the CO's station, protected by bullet-proof glass through which they could observe what went on in much of, but not all of the Sprung.

That day many of the kids were at the commissary buying candy and supplies. Of the students who remained, a few were lying on their beds napping and others were gathered in groups of three and four talking quietly.

The ceilings were so high that sounds were muted and seemed far away.

The skin of the Sprung, while it looked opaque from the outside, from within appeared to have a translucent quality. I remember there being a very nice sense of light and space in there.

I'd guess there were fifty beds spread out in a very meticulous grid, and most of them were well made. Whatever possessions the kids had were stored neatly beneath their beds. I was surprised that it appeared more like a boys' camp than a jail. But then I remembered how frequent the cuttings were and realized there was no place to hide. If both COs were, say, breaking up a fight in the bathroom—which could easily be a diversion—any number of assaults might be taking place out in the main hall. Or vice versa. I wanted to take a look at the bathroom, but, I have to say, I was afraid of what I might see—two kids had been headed that way as I was entering.

It didn't occur to me to check where the phones were. Whether the COs could see the phones from inside their station, I don't know. What I do know is that some students bragged about being on the phones for hours, while others were lucky to get calling privileges a couple of minutes a week. But even if phone time had been distributed fairly, being able to talk daily to your loved ones from jail would at best be surreal.

It seemed to me that an inmate would be better off if phones were an occasional privilege. Knowing that the person you're speaking to day after day is free and able to go about his or her business as usual while you're locked away and facing an uncertain future strikes me as cruel and unusual punishment. It would give one the illusion of freedom for a few moments at the end of which you're sent back to the slammer.

But it's not only by means of these modern "handles" that correction officers are able to exert nearly total control over the lives of inmates. They can also do this by meting out injustice the old-fashioned way, with their fists. There have been countless articles in the *New York Times* about that sort of treatment and worse. And there are numbers of documented cases of COs having inmates do that sort of dirty work for them on Rikers, though I never witnessed anything like that.

What I did see were two COs who seemed to get brutal once every three or four weeks. One of them was a fairly tall man who looked sensitive (but that may have been because he wore glasses). He was a Trinidadian of Indian descent. The other was an Italian-American who was probably five nine or so. Several days a week, the two of them worked as a team in the trailer I taught in. What struck me was that most of the time they both seemed like fairly nice guys. But every now and then the shorter man would have a bad day. When that happened, they would both beat on kids for minuscule reasons. I always felt that the taller man joined in during these moments to prove himself to his partner.

The shorter man usually sat with his legs up on the table in the hallway. His partner usually sat in a chair beside him with his arms and legs crossed. The shorter man seemed to be the leader. If a teacher sent a kid out of the room, sometimes the shorter man would smack the kid in the face. I never saw him punch a kid, but I've seen him slap kids on the face so hard that it must have hurt his hand and it definitely hurt the kid's face. Both COs would do this. I've seen them both knock kids to the floor and yell at them while standing over them, with one leg on either side of them. It was an entirely animal act.

Whenever I saw the COs behaving that way, I never knew what to do about it. The jail had all of the power and if they wanted, they could have kicked the school out indefinitely. And it wasn't as if the jail would have taken the word of a teacher over that of a CO. This was the most brutal setting I was ever in. But on Rikers, there never seemed to be anyone to whom I could complain. Though I witnessed a number of COs who were extremely dedicated and fair, I saw no one in power who seemed willing to buck the system—which is not to say that there weren't such people. I just never saw evidence of them.

If I had reported an incident of that sort, the two COs would have stood up for each other and my view would have been completely discredited. I even felt that if one of the brutalized students had been asked for his story, he would have come down on the side of the COs. If he hadn't, I suspect he would have paid dearly.

The school knew this sort of thing went on but they couldn't seem to do anything about it. There had been rifts between the school and the jail in the past, during which classes had been canceled. It may be that Jaynes and Cornwell stood up to COs who did this sort of thing, and that's what had led to the periods during which we did not have students. I never did find out.

*　*　*

One day a new kid kept falling asleep in my class. He had only been there a couple days and I was trying to get him engaged. We were reading *The Autobiography of Malcolm X*, and he kept putting his head on his desk and drifting off. I finally asked him what was wrong. He told me he had a headache. "Mister," he asked. "You got any aspirins?"

I told him I had some ibuprofen and asked if he wanted a couple. He said he did. I handed him two and he swallowed them without water and put his head back on his desk as the rest of us continued reading from *Malcolm*.

A few minutes later a CO walked past and through the window saw the kid sleeping. He stuck his head in and said, "Hey, you in the blue jacket. Wake up."

The kid sat up. The CO continued. "Don't let me catch you sleeping again."

The kid said, "The teacher gave me some pills and they're making me sleepy."

The CO looked at me. I told him my side of the story.

There were two times that I was reprimanded by the dep. This was the second. The first was when I was seen wrestling with Machete.

The world of Correction resembles the animal kingdom. Crime and Correction are two ends of the same violent stick. Out in the corridors and in the school, the kind of respect that's afforded a dep by other correction officers is visible, but not obsequious. But when you enter their inner sanctum, it's another matter. The dep's office is treated like a holy shrine. Correction officers don't enter unless they have an appointment.

When I showed up at the dep's office to be reprimanded, his sycophant told me to wait at the outer office while he went in to check that the dep actually wanted to see me. When he returned, he seemed disappointed to have to allow me passage.

The dep stood graciously as I entered his office. A little over six feet, he had a rugged build, a big head and an even bigger belly. Though he wore a distinguished pair of glasses, they did little to hide his jolly Irish face. When I first saw him, I thought he was older than he was, his hair being prematurely white. But soon it was clear that he was not even fifty.

He now greeted me with what I think of as a Roman salute: he held his right forearm across his chest parallel to his waist and he swung it out so that it was now pointing at me, his palm facing down the entire time. After that his hand remained out for me to shake. I never knew what he meant with this salute. I'd seen him salute people that way a number of times. It looked kind of fascist, but I decided it would be bad form to ask.

As I said, the first conversation I had with him was about wrestling with

Machete. I was just leaving the Sprungs on my way to lunch when I ran into him. He may have been on his way to see me. He stopped and told me he'd like a word with me. He was very friendly, but also quite serious as he warned me there in the hall that they would not renew my ID card if I continued to wrestle with students. This time, after telling me to be seated, he warned me across his desk that my ID card would not be renewed if I continued to provide medication to kids. In both cases I told him I realized I had made a mistake. Both times, he said he found my realization encouraging.

After we had completed that portion of the meeting, he asked me how I was doing and we shot the shit about our families and the like. After ten minutes or so, he stood, we shook hands, and I was on my way.

I was blessed with two parents who raised me to retain a sense of myself in situations of that sort. But most of my students were not as fortunate. I wondered what it felt like for them to meet with the dep for an appointment. I wondered how they were treated by the COs.

To the kids, the dep must have seemed like the owner of this plantation. Clearly the captain was the overseer. The warden was actually closer to being the owner, but most of the kids had probably never even seen him, whereas I would bet they saw the dep on a daily basis. To a fairly significant degree, he held their futures in his hands. He could reassign them, send them to the crazy house or to the Bing;[7] moreover, if he put in a good word with the DA, it could make the difference between getting out and hard time.

Leaving his office that day, I was reminded once again of how much more difficult my students' lives were than my own. Gurdjieff had this complicated notion that I will simplify, namely, the farther a person gets from his essential self, the greater is the number of cosmic laws under which he lives, that is, his life becomes increasingly complicated. It felt to me that my students were not only living under vast numbers of such laws while they were in jail: they were born under vast numbers of laws; they were born in the wrong place at the wrong time to the wrong parents.

What could they have possibly done to deserve their lot in life?
What could I have possibly done to deserve my easy life?

*　　*　　*

We were not supposed to bring cigarettes to the students. We weren't even supposed to bring candy. "Mules" is the term for people who smuggle goods in for inmates, and mules are not looked upon with favor by the DOC.

Many of our students had stopped going to school when they were ten, eleven—some even younger. They'd show up occasionally near the beginning of the year, but after that, many of them rarely attended. Sometimes, after they began selling drugs, they would stop by to make quick cash. Obviously an adult can't risk going into a school and selling drugs. But if he can get a kid to do it, he's safe. Not only that, he can do this in "good conscience." From his perspective, he's "only looking out for the kid." He's only making sure the kid has some money in his pocket. Not only that, the kid won't get punished as much as he would.

When our students had been in school, most of them had been a huge pain in some teacher's ass. Rikers was a kind of filter to gather all of those kids together into one school. Every classroom was full of world class pains. Kids like I was in school. So you're up there trying to teach, and suddenly everything you've been taught about teaching is completely irrelevant. It is time to improvise. I have the utmost respect for any teacher who could last on Rikers for as much as a month.

Out there it just so happened that the kids we were trying to teach didn't have any of the things that most kids take for granted. They didn't have candy. They didn't have their favorite type of soap. They didn't have combs or picks. They didn't have money. They didn't have cigarettes.

Now in a sense I'm exaggerating. They did have the possibility of having a commissary account to which their parents and girlfriends could contribute money and with which they could buy candy, soap, and cigarettes.[8] The problem was, many of them had no one back home who bothered to visit them or put money in their accounts so they had empty expense accounts. Their only means of getting supplies was to make deals with friends who did have money in their accounts or to steal from them.

Visitors were supposed to show everything to the COs that they intended to give to the kids. The kids were quite clever at making weapons out of the most apparently harmless items. Several times the captain came through and showed us samples of actual weapons the inmates had made. Kids would take an ordinary plastic toothbrush and file the end down by rubbing it on concrete until it had an incredibly sharp point.

They could do the same with a comb. I remember in particular a knife that had been fashioned out of a scrap piece of Plexiglas. It had the shape of a knife, including a handle wrapped in surgical tape to protect the user's hand. And as I already mentioned, a pencil made a lovely little weapon. It was sharp and the point would come off inside the victim's skin. Or eye, for that matter.

The beauty of these weapons, at least from the inmates' perspective, was that they could pass successfully through any metal detector anywhere. And because of the code that inmates follow, namely, "snitches get stitches," these weapons could be used with impunity. If you were an inmate and you saw someone stab someone else, when you were questioned you insisted that you were looking the other way when it happened. You heard a disturbance. By the time you looked around, all you saw was a kid holding his hand over his face and blood dripping out. There were twenty other kids standing there and you couldn't tell who had done it. The COs would hear this story from every kid, and a similar version from the victim, and after that, they'd bring in the turtles.

The turtles would turn the place upside down, knock kids around, search them as invasively as possible, and they'd usually turn up the weapon. But often, it would have been hidden in a place that made it impossible to connect to the individual who had used it.

So there was no way any teacher was going to bring in a comb or a toothbrush or anything with any substance to it. So if you were inclined to hand out a carrot of any sort, it pretty much boiled down to candy or cigarettes.

A certain percentage of kids—definitely a minority—didn't even smoke. But they all wanted cigarettes. Lacking access to money, their currency was cigarettes. So in giving them cigarettes you were in effect raising their status. That's how I rationalized it. At the time I still smoked and I knew how hard it is to go without cigarettes. It felt like an act of kindness.

After I quit smoking, I saw cigarettes completely differently. But during my final months in the Sprungs, I found them to be the most effective carrot available for a couple of reasons. First of all, as I said, they were money. Second of all, in giving them cigarettes I was breaking the rules which gave me a certain sparkle. The thing was, I was breaking a rule that no one cared about. COs sometimes saw me handing out cigarettes and they never said anything or complained to anyone.

The school probably would have frowned on it. But there were a lot of teachers who would not bring cigarettes but would bring candy and other junk that was nearly as harmful if not as provocative.

Later on, when I went over to the building, I didn't hand out anything and I looked back at myself and wondered how I could have been so stupid.

15. Why We Should Kill the White Man

There were many days when I would go home from school and write down a conversation we'd had in class. Without a voice recorder, doing that sort of thing with complete accuracy was impossible. The thing is, voice recorders were not allowed out there because of privacy concerns, but I would write down what I remembered of the class as well as I could.

Most of the time, I simply wrote down a situation or an exchange or two that had occurred during a particularly interesting class in hopes that I would later be able to recall the rest of the class. But there were classes that I attempted to recall from beginning to end, which was the case with the following one.

Some classes were more chaotic; others less. But I would say the feeling of three steps forward, two back, five forward, three back, was true much of the time in my classes on Rikers. There were other teachers out there who through force of will kept things moving in the right direction more effectively than I was able to do. When I tried that, I felt my control came at a cost. Somehow it seemed that I accomplished less on those days when I maintained the illusion of control. I did best when I maintained a fairly relaxed attitude and didn't try to force the situation as much.

This particular class took place a couple of weeks before a GED test, and it was a Friday. I had promised to bring two cigarettes for each kid who cooperated and participated in class that day. When possible, I preferred getting the computer with the large screen monitor from Mr. Cumberbatch, and we would write the essay on there. But that day, someone else was using it, so we did the essay on the blackboard. Two kids were there who had been there when I first started teaching out there, Tony and Metatron. Tony was still there, but Metatron had been released and had returned on another charge.

*   *   *

Just before I enter the room, Tony yells to the others, "Here he come now, that bald-head cracker."

He knows I can hear him, but he has to hide that he's the teacher's pet.

He has to hide it not only from the other kids, but from himself as well.

When I open the door, he says, "Yo, J-Dogg, where them bones at?"

Tony's about six three, big boned, strong, and very bright; moreover, he's been on the island for nearly a year and has acquired a lot of power. The other kids look up to him.

I say, "You'll get the bones as soon as you do some work. That was the deal. Two for everyone who works."

Tony acts like he's pissed, but beneath it all, there's a playfulness: "You be frontin', Jay. Word to mother. You just like every other White man."

"Frontin'?" I say. "The only one frontin' is you. The deal was first we work, then you get your bones. You know that."

Tony grins. He holds out his hand for a shake, says, "My main man, Jay."

I ignore him and look around the room.

He says, "You gonna leave me hanging, Jay?"

"Damned straight," I say, and everyone laughs—Tony too.

A kid named Raoul says, "You brought'm, Jay? For real? How many you brought?" Raoul's got a soft voice and he rarely says a thing.

"Two packs, just like I said. And only people who work will get them. And I'll be the judge of who's working."

Tony's all set to go. He's sitting up straight, looking alert. He says, "Ya'll mother fuckers shut the fuck up so's we can get us them bones. Come on, Jay. Teach us."

Everyone quiets down and I say, "We're going to practice writing an essay for the GED, and we're going to do it together, so it's going to be incredibly easy. All you have to do is..."

A kid by the name of Richard says, "If you want us to work, Jay, first you gotta show us them bones."

"I promise you—I have them right here in my bag."

"How we s'posed to know you ain't lying?" Richard says. He laughs. "Face it, mother fucker, you White."

Corey shakes Richard's hand and tells me, "He keepin' it real, Jay."

I pull the two packs of Newport 100s from my bag and hold them up. "Here they are. Still in plastic, just like when the good Lord made 'em."

Tony says, "My man, J-Dogg came through! And you brought them phat New Yorkers, Kid!"

By now Johnny's gotten up and he's coming over to examine the cigarettes up close. Johnny has the air of a kid used to getting his way. I tell him, "Yo, Johnny, sit down. You're not getting any bones until after the lesson."

Tony says, "Come on, J-Dogg. Let's get this shit out the motherfuckin' way so's I can get my bones, word up. What we learnin' 'bout today?"

"Like I already said, Tony, we're learning how to write an essay for the GED. And if you guys keep getting me off track, tough shit, by which I mean, no bones. I'm not fighting with ya'll today—that's why I brought the bones. It's Friday and I don't feel like fighting."

"You heard what the man said," Tony says. There's a note of panic in his voice. The kids quiet down and I continue.

"I thought maybe we could write an essay about capital punishment," I say. I know they'll object. The thing is, if I come in and ask them what they want to write about, they'll try to talk me out of writing at all, and I'll have to work harder to get anything out of them. This way the assumption is they're writing. The only question is what.

Tony is pissed. "Man, why you be bringin' in them boring ass themes? Why we don't be writin' about nothing interesting?"

Corey agrees: "Yeah, let us write about how to kill White people, things we need to know." Corey's fairly short, but you'd never know it from the way he carries himself. He's got a small face and the tops of his small ears are lower than his eyes.

"I thought you already know how to kill White people," I say.

"We do," Richard says. "That's why we want to write about it."

Tony says, "That's right. Back in the world, my teacher, she be saying that like every day: 'Write what you know.'"

"Word up, Jay," Johnny says. "Let us write about that and we'll be writing for days."

Richard says, "Won't take me no days: just write, 'Get you a Desert Eagle five oh and shoot the mother fucker in the head. The End.'" He wipes his hands together for emphasis.

Michael says, "Come on, J-Dogg, let us write about that."

In order for my scheme to work, I have to argue with them a little bit. Otherwise, they won't feel they've won—a lesson I learned from my mother, who was also a teacher.

"I don't know, guys," I say. "That's kind of radical. I could get in trouble allowing you to write an essay like that."

"Come on, Jay," Corey says. "Let us. We'll write good essays," He's practically whining.

"Here's the problem," I say. "Even if we were to write about that topic, most GED tests call for persuasive essays. And you can't easily write a persuasive essay about how to kill White people. That would be a process essay."

"You just scared we'll get ideas and use them on you," Corey says.

I tell him, "I'm willing to give it a try. But the problem is the way you've phrased the topic. How to kill the White man would be a how-to essay, and I've never seen a how-to essay on the GED. Figure out a way to rephrase it so you can write about it persuasively. In other words, it wouldn't be HOW to kill White people, but..."

Tony thinks he has it: "When to kill White people."

"Well, with a little finesse you could probably make that work. But what would be an easier one?"

"Why we should kill White people," says Corey.

"I guess that could work," I say. "So are you sure you'd rather write about that instead of capital punishment?" As I say it I can barely keep a straight face.

Richard has a better idea: "Let's write about why we should kill J-Dogg!"

"If you intend to kill me," I say, "bring your peoples. 'Cause you know I don't be playin'."

"Jay be thinking he Black."

"Jay be WISHin he Black.

Michael says, "You wish you was Black, Jay?"

"You want to know what I wish? I wish you guys would wake the fuck up and realize you're all a bunch of sinking ships and that if you don't start plugging the holes, you're going down."

Tony says, "Jay be buggin' today."

Corey says, "That's cause he didn't get him no pussy last night, right Jay!"

I say, "I think it's great that you worry about how much pussy I'm getting'. It's deeply moving. But if we're going to write this essay, we've got to get started."

Michael says, "I know you be eatin' the pussy, right Jay? 'Cause you got you that mad thick beard."

"Michael," I say. "When are you guys going to explain to me what a mad thick beard has to do with eating pussy. When will I get an answer?"

"I'm sayin' though," he says. "When you eat the pussy it make your beard thick."

"Jay know that already; he just be frontin'," Tony says. "So, Jay, the pussy still good as it was when I was back in the world?"

"No, Tony," I say. "The pussy has changed. Why do you guys always say

'THE pussy'? If you think there's only one of them, you've been here too long."

I spot a new student and I ask his name. He ignores my question and asks one of me: "Yo, Mister. What 'chu teach?"

"I teach English. My name's Jason. What's your name?"

He says, "So why you be talking like that?"

"Like what?"

"Why you be cursin' 'n shit. Teachers ain't s'posed to be cursin', especially English teachers."

I play offended. "Well, I'm cursing in English, ain't I. So what's the problem?"

"See, right there—'Ain't.' Real teachers don't say that. You ain't no real teacher."

"And you ain't no real student, so I guess we're even."

Everyone's laughing and the kid's looking around and getting pissed. He says to me, "Man, you's a stupid mother fucker."

I say, "Maybe. But smart enough to stay out of jail."

"Yeah? I see you out in the world, we'll see how smart you are 'n I put a cap in your ass." He's a short Black kid with a completely innocent face. In time, we'll become good friends. But first we have to go through the ritual. He's glaring at me and I have no doubt that if he had a weapon on him, he would give it his best shot.

Tony tells the kid, "Don't be messing with Jay. He'll smack flames out your ass; he know that Chinese shit."

I've begun handing out pencils and paper.

Tony says, "Hey, Jay, let me hand out the paper."

"Tony, just sit back down and let me hand out my own damned paper. Every time you hand it out, afterwards I'm missing half a ream."

"You sayin' I'm stealing from you? I thought we was cool, Jay. I thought you and me look out for each other. And now you saying I steal from you. Damn, Jay. That's some cold shit. And here I be fucking your wife for you on the regular. And you STILL be dissin' me like that."

"Oh," I say. "Is that you? She's been talking in her sleep about some guy with a little dick."

"Yeah," says Tony. "She told me about that guy too. She say his name is Jason."

I can't help but laugh at his quick response. I tell him, "Tony, you're lucky the COs are outside or I'd have to pull out on ya and give you a buck fifty 'cross your face, word up."

A buck fifty—that's when you cut someone so badly he needs a hundred fifty stitches.

"For real, Jay? You're gonna pull out on me? Where you be keeping your burner at?" Out in the world, a "burner" is a gun, but here it's a razor.[9]

"Right here," I tell him and I point to my mouth.

Tony says, "You be keepin' it in your mouth? So why you be sayin' you gonna pull out? You only say that when the burner's up your ass. If it's in your mouth, you s'posed to say 'I'll blow you up.' Ya'll White people can't talk our talk."

I say, "True true right right."

"See what I'm sayin'," Tony says. "You don't be sayin' it proper. You s'posed to say, 'True true right right.'"

"That's what I said," I say.

Richard says, "No, you said, 'True true right right."

"What's the difference?" I ask.

Now Tony is back on: "That's what we tellin' you. Y'all White people ain't smart enough to pick that shit up. But us brothers, we hear it."

Cory says to Tony, "Thank you," as if some great truth has finally been uttered that they shake on.

I say, "Well, since that's the case, let's get on with the lesson. Okay. So if you were taking the GED and the essay question was should we kill—who took my chalk?" I look around and I see it in Johnny's hand. "Johnny. Chalk please."

"I don't got your fucking chalk," he says. He's hiding it under his arm now and he shows me his empty hands.

"Johnny, chalk...I just saw it in your hand. Now give it to me... Thank you. Okay, so if you had to write a GED type essay asking should we kill White people, what would be the first thing you'd do?" I'm writing the question on the blackboard as I speak.

Now Corey complains. "Man, they don't be asking that shit on no GED."

"No shit, Corey. That's why I wanted you to write about capital punishment. But to tell you the truth, it doesn't matter. An essay's an essay. We could write about anything."

Corey says, "If it don't matter, let's write about my dick."

"No, that would be too short," I say.

Tony says to Corey, "Jay be dissin' you, Son."

Corey's looking to get back at me. He looks at the blackboard, "What's that say?"

"It says, 'Should we kill White people?'"

Corey says, "That's some sorry ass handwriting for a teacher, word up."

"Hey," I tell him, "come up and write it for me; that'd be great. Okay, so if the question were should we kill White people, what's the first thing you're going to do?"

Richard speaks: "Write, 'Yes. The end.'"

I hand Corey the chalk and I say, "But that's just an answer, Richard. For it to be convincing, you need details. Like if someone goes up to Tony and says, 'Yo, Ton. Your girl wants me,' and just leaves it at that, Tony's not necessarily going to believe him, right? But if he tells Tony, 'Yo, Tony, your girl called me last night and she told me her boyfriend's in jail and she's lonely and wants me to go see her,' etc., etc., at that point, Tony begins to realize his woman be playin' him. And that's because details are convincing, right Ton?"

Tony says, "Well you sure gonna like my girl pussy better than that stank ass thang your wife call a pussy."

"It's not me, Tony. It's some other guy."

David wants to know something. "So really, Jason: you eat the pussy?"

I say, "Check this out: David's got his hand in his pants and he wants to know if I eat pussy. You've been here too long, Son."

"I ain't your son," he says.

Out of the corner of my eye I see Johnny moving toward the desk where I've placed my bag. I tell him, "Yo, Johnny, step away from my bag."

"I'm just looking," he says. "Damn, this mother fucker's paranoid."

Corey says. "That's what I be telling all y'all niggas: that's cause he don't be gettin no pussy."

"How long you been in jail, Corey?"

"Six months."

"And you're worried about me not getting pussy? Come on, man. Who's not getting pussy? The only pussy you get is your hand."

"Well at least my hand's faithful," Corey says.

"That's not what I hear," I say.

Everyone laughs and Corey grins despite himself.

But David still has a burning desire to know one thing: "But Jay, you didn't answer my question. Do you eat the pussy?"

"Okay guys," I say. "That's Ms. Cornwell out there in the hall. For you new jacks, she's the assistant principal. So don't be blowin' up the spot."

Out in the world, 'the spot' is 'the drug spot,' and when you 'blow up the spot,' you do something that attracts the attention of the police.

I continue: "So we've got to stop talking about pussy. 'Cause if she comes in here and hears us talking about pussy, she might think we're talking about pussy. Know what I'm saying?"

Richard says, "The boy is scared to death."

Michael says, "She got you under mad pressure, right Jay?"

"She would have me under pressure if she heard us talking about pussy. Anyway, so what's the first thing you do before you even begin writing your essay?"

Tony says, "Indent."

"Even before that, what's the first thing you do? Come on, anyone..."

Tony guesses again: "You write the title."

"No, I'm talking about even before any of that shit."

Finally Tony gets it: "You make an outline."

"That's right. Very good, Tony."

"Do I get an extra bone?"

"No, but if you keep working like that, you'll definitely get both of them. So, yeah, we write a little outline. And how do we make an outline?"

Corey says, "You answer the essay question in a sentence and then you give two reasons for your answer."

"Excellent, Corey. So the question is should we kill White people? And of course your answer is 'no,' right?"

Richard thinks I'm serious. He says, "What?"

Tony says, "Stop frontin', J-Dogg."

I pretend to be surprised, or rather, I pretend to pretend. "Oh, so you think we SHOULD kill White people. Okay, so for our thesis statement, which is the opinion of our paper—the thing we're trying to prove—we write, 'We should kill White people.' Write that, Corey, please."

David says, "Man, this shit is boring. Let's talk about pussy."

I tell him, "David, pussy is not something you talk about. Especially when Ms. Cornwell is out in the hall. Okay, so we've answered the question. What do we do next?"

Corey says, "You give two reasons."

"That's right. You've got your opinion, that is, the thesis statement, and then you give two reasons for that opinion. And those two reasons will be the topic sentences of the middle two paragraphs also known as the what paragraphs?"

"Body paragraphs," says Tony.

"You believe this guy? Smaaarrrt! Damn! So, the body paragraphs are going to try to prove that opinion. So how many paragraphs are we going to have in all?"

"Four," says Michael.

"Excellent," I say. "And how will they be broken down?"

Corey says, "The first paragraph is the introduction, the second paragraph is about the first reason, the third paragraph's about the second reason, and the fourth paragraph's the conclusion."

"Damn, Corey, you are cooking today."

"I know you gonna hit me up with extra bones, right Jay."

"I don't know about extra bones, but keep it up and you'll definitely earn both of yours."

David says, "Yo, man, what about me?"

"Start talking about something other than pussy, David, and you'll get your bones too."

"Come on, Jay," he says. "Shit's rough. You should give us all extra bones. We doin' yo work."

I tell him, "First of all, David, it's not my work. It's your work. It's not going to help me, but it will help you. So pay attention and stop complaining. Not only that, shit's rough for Tony and Corey too. But look at them. They're some hard workin' mo-fo's. The GED is coming up at the beginning of next month, and I'm telling you, not one of you will pass that sucker without some work. So we've got to get moving."

Ms. Cornwell enters the room. I'm nervous about the sentence that Corey has written on the board about killing White people. Ms. Cornwell would not be amused by a sentence of that sort. She says, "Mr. Trask, may I have a word with you?"

"Tony says. "Look at him. He scared to death."

Ms. Cornwell looks at Tony and says, "He's got nothing to fear from me: he's an excellent teacher, don't you men agree?"

Tony says, "Word up, Ms. Cornwell. He be teachin' his ass off. That why he got him that little skinny White man ass."

"Young man!" Ms. Cornwell has a furious look on her face. You would swear she has never heard such foul language. "What is your name?" she asks. "Is that how you were taught to address faculty members in school?"

"No, Ms. Cornwell," Tony says sing-song. He's acting ashamed, but all of us can see he's only playing. Ms. Cornwell can see it too, but she makes believe his act is for real—it makes her job easier.

"It just slipped," he says. "That's cause I'm worried about my case."

Ms. Cornwell's face softens. "Well, just the same," she says. "You know better than to talk like that in school. Don't you?"

"Yes, Ms. Cornwell," Tony says. He hangs his head and now I'm wondering if maybe he really is ashamed.

She says, "I'm going to overlook it this once. But I don't want to hear language of that sort in this school again." Now she looks around. "Is that clear to all of you?"

In unison they all say with the utmost deference, "Yes, Ms. Cornwell."

Somehow they seem to find meaning in this game. The fact is, Ms. Cornwell has absolutely no power over them—no one in the school does. She can't give them so much as a detention. The correction officers are completely in charge of the kids. And though all of the kids and Ms. Cornwell are completely aware of the situation, they go through the motions in a way that somehow seems important. I don't know what's up, but I know it has something to do with Black womanhood. It's more than my cracker head can handle.

I know from the past that Ms. Cornwell is going to want to talk to me in the hall, so I grab my bag and walk over to her. She now says, "Mr. Trask, please step out here for a moment..."

Though she may not have power over them, she definitely has power over me. All sorts of power. She can fire me on the spot. I'm still on probation and will be until I complete several more education courses and become fully certified. We walk into the hall. She says, "I just wanted to ask you about the final you submitted for your class. I noticed that it only has one question, an essay question. Don't you also teach English?"

I said, "Well actually, Ms. Cornwell, I think of the essay as English."

"I mean grammar."

"Yes, I teach that too. But I teach the grammar as part of their overall writing. These guys have the GED coming up soon, so I figured I'd have them practice under test conditions for the essay."

"That's fine, but for the final, if you don't mind, I'd like you to have a variety of questions, true, false, multiple choice, those sorts of things. Okay?"

"Sure," I say. "I'll redo it."

"I would appreciate it if you would. And, if possible, please have it to me by the end of the day."

"No problem."

"Thank you," she says.

I return to the room and see that Corey has sat back down. Tony asks, "Yo Jay, what she be sayin'?"

"We were just talking about the final."

Michael says, "She got you under pressure, right?"

"Yeah, *mad* pressure," I say. "Let's get back to the essay question."

But first Tony has something on his mind: "Yo Jay—mind if I ask you a question?"

"You just did."

"Mind if I ask you another question?"

"You just did."

"Mind if I ask you two more questions?"

"Yes, I do mind. Let's get to work."

He's pointing at my pants and he says, "Where you get them ugly ass pants at?"

"We're not writing about my pants," I tell him.

"First tell me where did you get them."

"I got them at L.L. Bean, in Maine."

"L.L. Bean?" He looks surprised. "That shit be costin' mad loot, right? I thought they be stylin' at L. L. Bean."

"Some of their stuff is fairly stylish, I guess. But these pants I got at the factory outlet store in Freeport, Maine where they sell clothes that have defects in them. So I got these pretty cheap."

"You buy clothes with defects?" Tony can't quite believe what he's hearing—he wants to understand, but he just can't.

"Yes," I say. "They're cheaper that way."

"What's a defect?" Richard asks.

"A mistake," I say.

"What mistake?" Richard wants to know. He too is horrified. He seems concerned for me.

"I don't know," I say. "I wasn't able to find it."

"I know what it is," says Corey. "The mistake is that them pants was made."

"Why you so worried about my clothes?" I say. "I mean, here you are in jail and you're worried about my clothes. What's up with that?"

Tony says, "I'm sayin' though, Jay. Clothes is important. The clothes be sayin' to the world who you is."

"I can understand why you might think your clothes are important. But my clothes? Why you so worried about them?"

The new student sees an opening: "Yeah, well you claim to be a teacher, so you s'posed to be dressin' fly. You should be dressin' like us if you want us to listen to you."

"So you want me to buy pants that are too big for me so I won't be able to run from the cops because my pants'll be down around my knees. That's like a metaphor for why you're in here."

Saggin', by the way, like many of the styles that inundate our culture, supposedly got its start on Rikers when COs started taking belts away from inmates to prevent suicides.

Michael objects: "The cops didn't chase me, kid. I was up in my crib with my baby mama hittin' skins and we was mad blunted. Otherwise they wouldn't'a never caught me. That's word to my *grand*mother."

"The point is," I say, "most of you sold drugs to make money to buy clothes and shoes and you got caught and now you're in jail. So you're literally slaves to fashion."

Richard thinks he sees a subtle subtext to what I'm saying: "Yeah, we the slaves, and you the massa, right?"

I say, "So now I'm the master of fashion? Then why am I being criticized for being out of fashion? What I don't get is why you guys are so worried about what everyone thinks of you. What's up with that?"

The new student says, "I ain't worried about what no one thinks of me, Kid. That's why I'm here."

I say, "No, you're here precisely because you worry what people think of you: you need to live up to some image you want your friends to have of you. Just think about how many pairs of Timberland boots and Tommy Hilfiger sweatshirts you all have. And think about what you did to get those things."

Michael says, "Yeah, I'm not going to lie to you, Jay: I got over fifty pairs of Tims back in my crib. But that's only 'cause I like Tims, and not because of no one else."

"So it's just coincidence that Tims happen to be in fashion. Shit. I bet you in ten years when they're out of fashion, you won't be caught dead in them."

Corey thinks I'm full of shit. "They won't be out in ten years. Tims'll always be in."

"No they won't," I say. "Styles change."

"Not Tims."

"Soon you'll be making fun of people who wear Tims."

"Who told you that?" Corey asks. He seems nervous at the prospect of it. It's as if Tims are the very earth, rather than the shoes, on which he stands.

"Nobody needs to tell me that," I say. "I know it from experience. I can't believe you don't know it too. It's always that way with clothes."

"But not our clothes. They'll always be in."

"That's what every generation thinks about their clothes. You guys are too young to remember when people were wearing those Puma's and those Adidas shell tops. Everyone wore them. But no one wears them now. That's how fashion works. You'll see. And hopefully it will smarten you up to the ways that you've been jerked around by the man.

"The man gets on television and creates an image of how it's cool to wear this or that kind of shoes or sweatshirts or pants. And what do you guys do? You fall for that shit. And the thing is, you don't even seem to know it. Now that is some sad shit. You think you're fighting the man, but you're doing exactly what the man wants you to do. But anyway, let's talk about why you should kill White people. Okay, so we need two good reasons."

"Because he's alive," David says.

"Come on," I say. "Give me two good reasons. You've got to be convincing to people who don't necessarily agree with you. Two reasons."

Metatron has been sitting there patiently all period. He's been looking around and listening. He now speaks his mind: "Because the White man is the devil."

"Okay," I say. "But why's he the devil?"

"Because Mr. Yacub created him to be the devil."

"Who Mr. Yacub?" David asks.

I respond to Metatron: "That's just too simplistic for an essay. If you want to persuade someone, you have to..."

Metatron persists: "See, you don't want to know the truth. And you don't want us to know the truth. You just be frontin'. Whenever a brother starts talking truth around you, you just shut him up."

"Metatron, how's this: I'll give you a minute to explain about Mr. Yacub, okay? So everyone listen up. Metatron is going to tell us about how Mr. Yacub created White devils such as myself."

Metatron may be short, but he has grown in my mind to an impressive character. The kids call him a Five Percenter (as in, only five percent of the earth's population are righteous), but he calls himself a Poor Righteous Teacher. Whatever he is, he's part of a radical offshoot of the Nation of Islam. He may not think his own thoughts, but somehow he *is* his own man.

When he starts speaking about his religious beliefs, his grammar changes and his enunciation becomes stylized. He now says, "The many think that the White man is the devil because he does evil. But as usual, the many are wrong. The truth is, the White man does evil because he is the devil. He was created to be the devil, to be the expression of evil on earth. Evil is the White man's nature just as good is Original Man's nature. The White man is the Grafted Man, grafted by Mr. Yacub.

"Yacub created this Grafted Man many years ago on the Island of Patmos. Mr. Yacub traveled there from Africa and took with him a small group of Black men and women from whom he created the brown man. He knew that within each Black man there was one Black gene and one brown gene, so he bred the Black people in such a way that they had brown babies. And when these babies grew up, he bred them until he created the red man. And then he took the red men and bred him until he created the yellow man. And then he took yellow man and bred him until he created the White man, and the White man is the devil. He is the devil because he is so far removed from what God created, which was Original Man, the Black Man.

"After creating this devil, Mr. Yacub took him back to Africa and used him to cause mischief among Original Man. But Original Man was not fooled by the Grafted Man and threw him out. Grafted Man went up to Europe where it was the ice age and he lived in caves.

"The White man does everything in his power to hide all this. And one of the things he does is undermine Original Man's confidence in himself. For instance, he refers to Original Man as a Negro, trying to brainwash the Black man to believe that he is not as developed as the White man. The word "Negro" is made from the words "Needs" and "Grow," implying that Original Man 'needs to grow.' All of this is part of the brainwashing done by the Grafted Man."

Michael is curious. He asks Metatron, "Where you hear that at?"

"From Allah—Arm, Leg, Leg, Arm, Head."

"What?" Michael seems confused.

Metatron repeats it: "Arm, Leg, Leg, Arm, Head. Those initials spell 'Allah,' the one true God."

Michael now asks me, "That shit true, Jason?"

"You mean, am I the devil?"

"Yeah."

"It doesn't work to ask the devil if he's the devil. He'll just say no. So, come on, let's get to get to work on our essay."

"No, let's talk about this," David says.

"What do you guys want? To write the essay and get bones or talk about Mr. Yacub and get no bones?"

"See, he's trying to hide the truth from us brothers," says Metatron. "That's how Grafted Man's mind works. He's only teaching out here so brothers won't hear the truth. That's cause Grafted Man knows that in jail, the Black Man is more likely to hear the true teachings of Allah than anywhere else. So Grafted Man makes sure he comes in here to interfere."

"What are you talking about?" I say. "I just let you finish an explanation of how I'm the devil, and then when I try to get the class back on track..."

"You only did that to try to make it look like it's not true."

"I can't argue with you, Metatron. No matter what I say, you'll just say it's part of some scheme. How many times have we been through this already? Look at what I'm trying to do. I'm trying to help you guys so you can write an essay that will enable you to pass the GED. Without an education, kids will just end up back in here again. Okay," I say to the class. "Two reasons why we should kill the White man."

"Because he causes so many problems."

"Yeah, that works, Cory. Come back up here and write it on the board, if you would. So now we need just one more reason."

Tony says, "Because he always causes problems."

"That's too close to the other reason. Let's try to come up with two distinct reasons so that we'll have two completely different body paragraphs."

Richard suggests, "Because the White man had his chance and he blew it."

"That might work," I say. "We'll put it up here and we'll see if it works when we try to come up with examples. But it's definitely okay for our working outline. Corey, you'll have to write larger so everyone can read it. So what will we use for our first sentence?"

"I think we should kill the White people."

"Yeah, that's a possibility."

David's drawing and he doesn't appear to be listening. I say, "Hey, David. Please pay attention. So, like I said, that's a possibility. But there are better ways. Any suggestions?"

I wait. When no one speaks, I say, "How about describing the situation with the White man today. Instead of giving your opinion up front, first describe the situation and then give your opinion about it. For instance, you could talk about the fact that nearly everyone in this jail is either Black or Hispanic and how that's proof that the White majority in this country is racist. And, by the way, is that something that's true only in America?"

"No," Michael says. "White people be doin' that shit all over the world."

"Right," I say. "So you can add that too, which is ultimately Metatron's point."

"Don't say that's my point because it's not. My point is that the White man is the devil, not that he just happens to do bad things. He does bad things because he is the devil. So don't be mixing your lies with the truth."

"Fine. That's NOT Metatron' point. So what does it prove that White people are doing this stuff all over the world?"

Richard said, "That it's not just American crackers."

"Okay," I say. "So after we write all that, we introduce the thesis statement, which is the opinion of the paper."

David's frustrated. "Yo, Jay, what the fuck opinion you talking about?"

Tony says, "That we should kill White people."

"My man Tony comes through," I say and we shake. "Okay. So that's how you're going to do your first paragraph. So why don't you take a couple of minutes and write it out on your paper."

"What?" Richard says. "I thought you said we was writing it together."

"Come on, Richard. We are writing it together. We just did the first paragraph together. Now you're going to write your version of it on your paper to make sure you know how to do it."

"That's that bullshit."

"You better start writing, Richard. Time's a wasting."

The new kid says, "You be stealin' that shit from Bugs Bunny."

"What? Oh, 'Time's a wasting'? That's right. That's from Bugs."

"You not s'posed to steal. I thought you was a teacher. That's plagitism."

"It's not plagiarism. I was quoting."

"I don't see no quotation marks."

"Okay," I say. "So you're blind. Don't worry about it. Instead worry about getting those bones. If you want them, you'd best be writing."

Reluctantly he picks up his pencil and begins. I walk around and check to see that kids know what they're doing. I wait a couple more minutes and they finish up.

When most of the kids have finished, I say, "Okay, why don't you read me what you have, Tony."

"Look around this mother fucker," he reads. He's breathing fast and I can tell he's a little nervous but also proud of what he's written. "You see any White boys? Me neither. What's up with that? Why is it that Black kids and Puerto Ricans are here but no White kids? I'll tell you why. Because crackers is a bunch of racist mother fuckers and we should kill them all."

"That's not bad for a first draft," I say. "Now, on the GED exam, what would happen if you wrote words like 'mother fucker'?"

"They'd fail your ass," Corey says.

"I think that's probably true. If you were extremely lucky, you might find an enlightened scorer who would be open enough to get beyond words of that sort. But hopefully none of you are going to find out, right? Anyone got any other suggestions for improving Tony's introduction?"

David says, "Well, he says, 'Look around this mother fucker,' but he don't say what this mother fucker is."

"Very good, David. That's exactly right. So how could he fix it?"

"He should tell us what this mother fucker is."

"Excellent. Anything else?" I wait.

No one says anything so I recap: "So basically, Tony, you should mention that you're talking about being on Rikers, you should get rid of the profanity, and maybe add a sentence or two to beef it up a bit."

"What am I s'posed to add?" Tony wonders. "I said it all."

"Another detail or two. Maybe something about how long you've been here and how many kids have come through the system in that amount of time and yet you haven't seen more than one White kid during that entire time, or whatever."

"See, there he goes," says Metatron. "He's trying to soften what Tony wrote. Tony be sayin' there are no White people here, but Grafted Man tries to make it seem like there are some White kids here, just not as many."

"Metatron," I say. "There was a White kid here last month in this very classroom—remember? The other Tony? White Tony?[10] If there's only been one White kid in here during the past three or four months, that doesn't undercut Tony's argument.

"So, Tony, if you mention jail as the setting, get rid of the profanity and add a couple more details, you'll be golden. Okay, so the second paragraph?"

"Write about the first reason," says Corey.

"Which is?"

"Because he causes so many problems."

"That's right, Corey. So we begin with that reason and what are we going to write about after that?"

"An example of the problems."

"Right. I just noticed that we don't have much time left, so we have to hurry. So what are some examples of the problems? Any suggestions, Metatron?"

"He deceives and he lies."

"Okay. What would really be good would be if you were to give specific instances of the White man's deceiving and lying?"

"He promises but does not deliver."

"Good. And a specific promise that he has not delivered on? Anybody. The more specific we make the example, the better. And the more it gives us to write about."

"Well," says Tony. "Dr. Steele be sayin' that Black people in America got promised forty acres and a mule after that war, there."

"Good," I say. "That's a perfect example. So you would write that some of the problems that he causes have to do with making promises he doesn't keep. And then as an example you write about how following the Civil War, newly freed slaves were promised forty acres and a mule by General Sherman, and the White American government never kept that promise. What's another example that you could write about? And remember, you don't have to limit yourselves to examples of the White man lying, though that's fine to do. You could also write about violence that the White man committed, or any sort of trouble they've caused."

"What's this 'they' shit," Richard says. "Just say 'we.'"

"Okay, any problems that WE have caused. Any suggestions?"

"Making Black people into slaves."

"Very good," I say. "And you could include the Middle Passage, the murder of slaves, the mistreatment, the miserable conditions in which slaves were kept, the way slaves were not allowed to learn to read and write, etc., etc. So you could write about any or all of that in your first body paragraph.

"Okay, so your next reason is 'Because the White man had his chance and he blew it.' What examples would you use for that one? Come on, David. Tell us what you're thinking."

"The White man been in control for a long time and he been treatin' the Black man like shit."

"Okay. But again, let's make it a bit more specific."

David tries again: "He been running things since forever and he still treat the Black man like shit."

"The problem is that both of those sentences are more or less a repeat of 'he had his chance and he blew it.' Let's come up with a specific example of how he treated the Black man like shit."

"Slavery."

"I think we have a problem with this reason. Basically, it's too close to the other reason. If we use this reason, we'll end up with two identical body paragraphs. You see what I'm saying?"

"Why don't you be tellin' us that before?"

"I wasn't sure about it before. I did say that we'd have to see if it works or not."

"You didn't say that," Corey says.

I'm tempted to remind him that I'd said it was good enough for a working outline. The thing is, I'd be wasting my time because Corey has never lost an argument in his life. Instead I say, "This is the way essay writing often goes. You come up with a reason, and when you begin writing about it, you sometimes realize it doesn't work. So you try again. Anyone got a better reason, one that will allow us to use different examples from those in the previous paragraph?"

"There ain't no other reason," Tony says.

"You telling me that you can only think of one reason to kill the White man? It sounds to me like the White man might talk his way out of it." I wait. "How about this?" I say. "What if we change the first reason slightly. Instead of 'Because he causes so many problems,' how about we make it 'Because he causes so many problems for Black people.' That way, in the second body paragraph we'll be able to write about problems he causes for other people. What do you think about that?"

"True true right right," says Richard.

"So what's an example of the way he's treated other people?" I ask.

"He dropped the atomic bomb on them Chinese," Corey says.

"Japanese," I say. "But yeah, that's true. Good. What else has he done?"

"Didn't he lock them Japanese up in jails?" the new kid says.

"That's right. Very good. The internment camps during the Second World War. Absolutely. What else has he done to people in this country?"

"He killed the Indians."

"Very good. There are other examples as well that we could come up with. Not only that, we don't have to limit it to American Whites. We can include all Whites. So what else has the White man done? Anyone think of anything else that happened during World War Two?"

"Yeah," the new kid says. "Them Nazis be killin' the Jews."

"Very good," I say. "Sounds like someone knows his history. So if you use two of those examples and go into detail, you'll definitely be able to come up with a very solid paragraph. We've only got five minutes left, so let's talk about the conclusion. What do we need to accomplish in the conclusion?"

"You finish it up," Tony says.

"Good. And how do you do that?"

"You say the same tired shit you say in the first paragraph."

"Well, Corey, to a degree that's true. You ram home the point you're trying to make. And what point are you trying to make?"

"That we should kill the White people."

"Right. And then what else are you going to try to get across?"

"Why we should do that."

"Exactly. So is that it?"

"Yes. Give us our bones," Tony says.

"There's one more thing. What is it?"

"Our motherfucking bones," Tony says.

"There's one more thing you need to do in that conclusion. What is it?"

"End the mother fucker so we can get our bones."

"Well that's close, Tony. What you need to do is make it feel like an ending."

"That's what I said. Now give us our fucking bones."

"First, I want you to listen for a couple seconds. On the GED, when you're given an essay question to write about, what's the first thing you do?"

"Make a motherfucking outline," Tony says.

"Which consists of what?"

"Your opinion and two reasons."

"Good. Tony, let someone else answer the next question. How do you structure the first paragraph?"

"Structure?"

"Yeah, how do you write it. What comes first?"

"Your opinion," says Tony.

"Only if you don't mind being lame. What comes first?"

"The situation you're writing about."

"Tony, let someone else answer. And what's the last thing you write in the first paragraph?"

"Your opinion."

"Tony knows it. Do the rest of you know it? Why do you let Tony look like he's the man? What's the first thing you write in your second paragraph?"

"First reason."

"Good, Corey. And then what do you write?"

"Examples."

"Great. And your third paragraph?"

"Your second reason and examples," says Richard.

"So what about your last paragraph, the conclusion?"

"Same as first paragraph," says Johnny.

"Not quite. What goes into the concluding paragraph?"

"You make it feel like an ending," says Tony.

"Good. But before that?"

"You give your opinion and your reasons."

"Great, Corey, but be sure to word that last paragraph differently from the way you worded the first paragraph so it doesn't just feel like an instant replay. If you remember all this stuff and if you actually do it, you've got a good chance of passing the writing portion of the GED. We'll practice more next week. And when we do, I'm going to give you a question and you'll do the essay by yourselves so that we can see where you all are. So here are the cigarettes I promised."

As I open up a pack, I tell them to hand me their pencils as I hand them their cigarettes.

"Phat New Yorkers," Tony says.

"Why do you call them New Yorkers?" I ask as I hand them out.

"That's how we do."

"Why do you smoke menthol, anyway. I don't understand that. I can't stand menthol cigarettes. Sit down, Michael. If you want your cigarettes, sit down."

"Why I gotta sit down?" he says.

"Because I saw what you did last time I brought cigarettes in. You got your cigarettes then moved to the other side of the room and tried to get two more, so sit down if you want your cigarettes. Michael, where's your pencil?"

"I gave you my pencil."

"Oh, so that means you already got your cigarettes."

He hands the pencil over.

"How is it that an entire jail smokes Newports?" I ask. "What's up with that? Everyone sit down. I'm giving you two apiece and that's it. So stay seated so I know who I've already given them to. Tony, sit down. Anyone who's standing won't get bones."

"Thanks, Jay," Corey says.

"Yeah, thanks, Jay," several of them say at once.

"Have a good weekend, guys," I say.

Michael comes over and holds out his hand. "Ain't you gonna hit me up, Jay?"

I tell him, "I already got you, Michael."

One of the correction officers blows a whistle and I say, "Take care guys."

"Bye, Jay," Johnny says.

They go stomping out into the hall to line up. I notice that Tony is hanging back. After everyone else has left the classroom, he comes over to me and says, "Your name in the phonebook, J-Dogg?"

I tell him it is. "Good," he says. "Cause I ain't seen your wife and my kids in the longest." He then grins and bro-hugs me, tells me he has court the next day, that he'll probably be going home. He promises to give me a call.

"Thanks for teaching us, Jay."

He shakes my hand again and leaves.

*　*　*

Tony actually did call me. I recognized his voice immediately. I don't know what happened, but soon after we started talking, I heard some sort of background noise, as if someone was talking to him. He told me he had to go. We hung up without exchanging contact details. He called my home phone and we didn't have caller ID. I was hoping he would call me again, but he never did. I wish I'd arranged to meet him for coffee. I wish I could remember his last name so I could look him up on Facebook. By now, I suspect Tony has his act together.

16. Teachers

Maybe six months before I left the Sprungs Mr. Nussbaum began teaching there. I believe he would have been six five if not for what looked like curvature of the spine. He was skinny as you can be and still walk. Were I making a film, I would cast him as the lead character in "The Hunger Artist." He certainly wore more clothes than Kafka's character—dark suits several sizes too large that he must have picked up at Goodwill along with Soviet drab shirts and dark ties. His hair was all the same length, maybe three inches, just long enough to begin to curl and he more or less slicked it back.

He wore some sort of bracelet—it might have been a medical bracelet for asthma or hemophilia. I never got a close enough look at it. But I did notice that it was much too big and forever sliding up and down his forearm, sometimes over his shirtsleeve.

He wouldn't make eye contact with anyone and when you greeted him he wouldn't utter a sound. In fact, he seemed to close his eyes when you did so, which at first struck me as shyness. I found myself pitying him, wondering how he could possibly face a classroom of our kids. But the more I inspected him—and I spent considerable time doing so because I am after all nosey and curious and easily puzzled—the more I realized that the shy model did not account for much of his behavior.

After greeting him a number of times, it seemed to me that his way of closing his eyes was his way of communicating stubborn irritation. It was as if he'd made up his mind not to be bullied by the assholes of the world who insist on saying 'hello' to everyone. There was something of Raskolnikov about him. Or possibly Bartleby. Yes. In fact, that's who I would cast him as—not as the hunger artist, but as a latter-day Bartleby.

Just so it's clear, I sympathized with him one hundred percent. I truly believe that a person has a right not to do what's expected of him by the rest of society so long as he is not hurting anyone, and he clearly was not. But I have to say that seeing someone so unsociable on Rikers Island where kids are completely ruthless to everyone—yeah, it struck me as strange.

There was something about Nussbaum that made you not want to cross him. In fact, his demeanor was such that you were forced to respect him.

For that reason, as far as I know no one ever went in to observe him teaching.

We could see him through the window from the hallway, but that was it. Surprisingly enough, from that perspective, he seemed to do fairly well. The kids paid attention to him. I can't imagine that any of them would trust themselves to ask him the sorts of questions they asked me about myself and my wife and kids and the rest of it. But they may have.

I'd walk past his window and look in and the kids would be sitting there watching Nussbaum write on the board, or he'd be talking and they'd be listening. Who knows what he was saying. He always had a serious look on his face and the kids looked serious too. Even kids who were total clowns in other people's classes would sit there listening. And it didn't look as if they were just being polite. They seemed interested. I wondered if he was telling them something about life the rest of us had overlooked.

The kids didn't say anything about him to the rest of us. I wasn't sure if it was loyalty or what. Maybe they were protecting him. I never figured it out. There was no predicting how someone would do on Rikers. Watching him made clear that there are many ways of being a successful teacher in an alternative educational setting.

*   *   *

Two young men, Guy and Hernandez, started at about the same time. Guy was a young Black man whose brother was a CO in the building. Now, whereas Guy was short and skinny, his brother, Marvin, was about six six and a champion weightlifter. He was solid muscle. He looked like a professional fullback or something. Teachers in the building told a story of him picking up two inmates by the neck, one in each hand, and walking down the hall with their feet dangling. Though that story may not cast him in a favorable light, of all the COs who worked with our students, Marvin was the one who encouraged them most to get a good education. He was a huge asset to the school.

Stature was just one of the reasons it was difficult to see how Guy and Marvin had been born from the same woman. Guy often presented himself as a bit helpless. His mantra seemed to be that if you get everyone to sympathize with you, your life is easier. Whatever it was, it went over well with Ms. Jaynes and Cornwell. At one point they had him basically running the Sprungs. This was after Rhodes had left and after Dr. Steele had fallen out of favor with them. While he was lead teacher in the Sprungs, he did a lot to protect us, just as Rhodes had. Both men stood up to The Ladies. Steele and Cornwell in particular did not get along.

When Dr. Steele's father died, it hit him quite hard. He stayed out of school for five or six days, which we all thought was understandable. When he came back we learned that Ms. Cornwell had called him after four days and told him it was time he came back to school, that he needed to act like a man and get on with his life.

Most of us in the Sprungs felt The Ladies were threatened by Dr. Steele's leadership. It was after his dismissal as lead teacher that the power vacuum was filled by Guy.

Guy was a para-professional, which was basically the same as an assistant teacher. But out there, like everything else, the position was ambiguous. Though no one referred to him as our leader, he was the one who brought word from on high—from The Ladies and DOC. And he was the man we had to go to for information.

Over all, he was a good person, but at that point in his life, he was not qualified for a position of that sort, not only because he was inexperienced and lacked the training and education, but he was also immature and held grudges.

The months of Guy's reign, I suspect, were The Ladies' way of teaching those of us in the Sprungs a lesson. It was the period of the lowest morale that I witnessed while on the island.

Guy was arbitrary and if you even rolled your eyes at him, he was liable to get even with you. I liked Guy and I used to give him rides, but occasionally I would let him know when I felt he was being petty. He'd act sad for a while when he saw me. Guy definitely knew his way around a stage.

It appeared that Guy was in charge of Henriquez. Some days, Henriquez would complain all the way to school about Guy, and at night on the way home, if Guy rode with us, Henriquez kept quiet.

Henriquez was also hired as a para-professional. He was about twenty-one years old and he had recently moved up from the Dominican Republic. His English was slightly better than my Spanish which is non-existent. We found out that we lived a few blocks apart and he began riding to Rikers with me. I'd wait out at the end of North Fifth and Roebling and he'd walk up and meet me. Every day he'd get in and shake my hand as if we hadn't seen each other in a decade. His greeting was always the same:

"Know what I'm shaying?" in imitation of the Eeyore student we both knew. We'd laugh about it and off we'd drive to Rikers.

Henriquez had an innocent sort of charm about him and an infectious laugh. His laugh could also be inappropriate. It was as if he had no conception that the person he was laughing at knew what was up.

One time the two of us were standing at an intersection of hallways waiting for a file of inmates to pass. One of the inmates had the smallest head I've ever seen, but with normal-sized facial features crammed onto it. When Henriquez saw him he said to me, "You see him, that bastard? He have a teeny head!" He laughed. I tried to shush him because the guy was only a few feet away from us. Henriquez didn't seem to understand what I was doing. He kept repeating himself enthusiastically, "Hey, Jay. You see that teeny head bastard?" The way he implored me to look was so innocent it was frightening.

It was clear to everyone except those in charge that Henriquez, his personal charm notwithstanding, was not qualified to work with students, though, to his credit, he did fairly well in the Spanish speaking classroom.

One day he was left in charge of a classroom because a teacher was out and there wasn't a sub to cover the class. A Black kid was giving him shit and Henriquez got pissed off and called him a monkey. The kid called Henriquez a racist and Henriquez just kept repeating that the kid was a monkey. All of the teachers were aware of it, but nothing was done about it. After I left, I'm told he was suspected of bringing in a razor blade to a Dominican kid who had been sliced across the face by a Black kid. After that they let him go.

There was another incident with a razor blade. Mr. Stryker and I were on our way back from the cafeteria, and, as with Henriquez, we were waiting for a file of inmates to pass. When Stryker reached into his pocket to pull out his wallet, a razor blade slipped out and fell to the floor. About twenty feet away from us stood a dep talking to a CO. Stryker stood there frozen in fear. I whispered to him, "Put your foot on it." He did.

I knew why he had the razor blade. He was an art teacher and it was nearly impossible to find anything to cut materials with. Cutting devices were *verboten* and if you tried to bring in anything other than a razor blade, when you passed through the metal detector it would go off and you'd be searched. The metal detectors through which inmates passed were set on an extremely high level so that even the smallest bit of metal would set them off. But the metal detectors that COs and teachers passed through were set at a far lower level so that our belt buckles and zippers would not set them off.

After putting his foot over it, Stryker still looked confused about what to do. He finally turned his back to the dep. He leaned over and in the process of tying his shoes, he picked it up. If he had been caught with it, I suspect he would have lost his job.

And then there was Mr. Henie, the White guy to whom Ms. Jaynes and Ms. Cornwell introduced me on my first day. He would come out to the Sprungs from time to time to encourage our students to submit writing to his magazine. On days like that, he would go around with me to my classes. Unlike most of the teachers who had lasted out there, Henie was not what you'd call an intense person, but he did well with the kids just the same. He had something they wanted, a magazine in which he might publish their stuff. He would come into a class with me and I'd introduce him. He'd hand out copies of a previous magazine of kids' writing that he'd put together and go over some of the stories and poems kids had written, some of whom my students knew.

Henie would read a poem and a kid would say something about the author such as, "I know that kid. He stay on my block."

Mr. Henie would tell the students that if they wrote something that the magazine published, he'd give them copies to send home to their mothers and girlfriends. Suddenly kids would see themselves as writers. He'd tell them they could write a poem, a rap song, a story, or even an essay. He'd collect writing that he considered finished and have students continue working with me on pieces that needed work. After they had gotten their pieces to shine, I'd take them over to him.

He worked in the building, so when he showed up at the Sprungs twice a year or so, he seemed like a rather exotic fellow. Many of the kids felt that they had failed as criminals because they were in the Sprungs rather than in the building. So when anyone came over from the building, the kids were impressed.

Later Mr. Mitchell came along and he did the same thing in the Sprungs that Mr. Henie did in the building. He was very gentle, but because he was such a bear of a man, he was not someone whom the kids felt they could push around. They clearly respected him.

He was a talented poet and prose writer. He had been writing for a long time and when he did public readings he sometimes had a jazz band backing him up as he read, the way the Beats used to do it. He was the sort of

Black man the kids had only seen in films. He was able to get a lot out of them.[11]

Not long after that, we got a second art teacher in the Sprungs. Mazovich was a White guy in his early thirties who wore his hipness on his sleeve. He was a good guy, but he had this thing about being hip: if it was hip, he was all over it. The hip New York club and art scenes. Hip music. Hip theater. Hip photography. Hip words. He had this bisexual persona going on. He would wear shirts that were unbuttoned down to his navel. He would go into these burlesque soliloquies about his nipples that were very funny. He would grab them and make all manner of pouting faces.

Occasionally he would go into the classroom in that mode and I worried that he would have problems. The kids on Rikers were in an extremely precarious position and they were wild and I wondered how his particular way of going through the world would affect them.

He did just fine. In the end, he confirmed my feeling that the most effective way of approaching the kids, as is true in any classroom, is to just be yourself. If teachers tried to hide anything about themselves the kids would sense it and give them hell. The only type of teacher they absolutely could not stand was someone who was not themselves, i.e., teachers who do things the way they're taught to, the so-called "professionals." Watching Mazovich, I began to understand how Beedy felt when he heard that I was using my first name with the kids.

Beedy, by the way, during my second year, ended up not returning after the April vacation. We all kept asking where he was and it finally came out that he had a crack problem and he'd gone on a bender. He had a lot to live up to. His father had been a career military officer and I don't think he ever felt that he could possibly "be the man his father was." He never returned after that.

One thing I'll say for The Ladies is that after he failed to show up, for over a month they tried to get him to return. They offered to help him find a way out of his addiction. But I suspect he was too proud, knowing that by then we had all heard what had happened to him.

17. God, Dildos, Race & Thanksgiving

For the most part, White and Black staff members got along. This does not mean, on the other hand, that there was much interaction between the two groups. Getting along is easy when you don't have a relationship.

And just so it's clear, it's not as if the White people on the island were trying to make friends with the Black people. Nor were the Black people hoping to hang out with the White people. In my opinion, both groups were difficult. We were, after all in New York City, and no one does difficult like New Yorkers.

Every now and then one or another of my White friends on Rikers would say something that made me realize I was seen as bending over backwards to keep Black people happy. I don't believe it was a case of them having hostile feelings toward Black people, per se. It's just that they were ultimately New Yorkers. And one of the basic mantras of New Yorkers is—and it doesn't matter if they are White or Black—"If someone doesn't understand you, tough shit for them." The idea is that there are plenty more people who *will* understand you. So move along and find those people. That attitude complicates things, in a place like New York City, when there's a misunderstanding between a White person and a Black person. It increases mistrust all around.

Except for a couple of days when my car broke down, I always drove to Rikers, and on the way home, I usually gave several people rides to one of several subway stations. At various points I gave rides to Beelman, Jim, Bill, Rumi, Henriquez, Mazovich, and Guy. By the last year I was there, I had a Crown Vic we inherited from my wife's uncle. The thing had a bench front seat. I was giving rides to up to five, sometimes six people at a time. Rumi and Guy were Black. Henriquez was Dominican. The others were White. Some afternoons a near race riot would break out in the car. On the face of it, race had nothing to do with it. But it seemed to me that racial tension was behind it. For instance, it seemed to me that Rumi felt Bill was prejudiced against Black people and that Bill felt Rumi was prejudiced against Jews. I felt caught in the middle some afternoons when the arguments got started.

One time, I got into an argument with Rumi—who in time became one of my best friends—and he still is. The next time I saw him, he treated me coolly. Then when I saw him again, I said, "What's going on, Rumi?" I don't think he would have minded the fact that we argued if Bill hadn't been there. But the fact that he *was* there made Rumi feel somehow that I had sided with Bill against him. Bill hadn't taken an active part in the argument, but one time he did say something that backed up my point.

I reminded Rumi that several times in the past I had sided with him against Bill. We talked our way through it and got our friendship back on track. After that, whenever an argument of any sort began in the car, I stayed out of it, which is not something that has ever come easy to me.

*   *   *

A race relations group came to work with the faculty. On Wednesdays, we would see our students in the morning, and then after lunch, the group would come and we'd get down to work.

This was the best group of its kind I have ever seen, including an excellent group I witnessed in the army. They spoke to us about things that made people completely uncomfortable. They spent a lot of time getting us to talk about our own suspicions about what other races and genders thought about our race and gender. For instance, White people believing that Black people felt White people should kiss Black ass to make up for all the past abuse. Black people feeling that White people thought they were superior to Black people. Hispanic people being suspicious that Whites and Blacks thought Hispanics were stupid. Women being suspicious that if men were nice to them it was because they wanted their bodies. Men being suspicious that women thought men were knuckle-dragging brutes.

They had us role-play to show how deeply ingrained these suspicions were and how they affected our dealings with each other. These interactions were often quite funny, yet they enabled us to see many of the attitudes that we hid from ourselves but were obvious to everyone else.

In one exercise, we had an imaginary line running through the middle of the room. Half of the faculty was placed on one side of the line; the other half, on the other side. We were each stationed across from a person of a different race and/or gender and we were told to hold the right hand of that other person. The object of the game was to get the other person onto our side of the line through talking alone.

I was placed across from Ms. Peterson, a Black woman. She was a veteran teacher out there and she was six or seven years older than I. I tried to convince her that we could have a win/win situation if we would both move to the other person's side at the same time, but to do so, would involve putting faith in the other person.

She wasn't hearing it. She said she didn't believe for one second that I would actually move to her side. She feared she would end up on my side and I wouldn't move, and then at that point, I would "win." We were both laughing about all of this, but she wasn't about to budge.

I said, "How about if we both move simultaneously and we do it in slow motion. We can support each other by grabbing each other's forearms, and we can move our feet slowly to the other side and we'll do it at the same exact time."

She would hear none of it. She wanted me to move to her side and she said that I wanted her to move to my side. She said I was just being sneaky. Despite our laughter, I could not get beyond her suspicion. That was the beginning of us becoming good friends. Later when I went over to the building to teach, I sought her advice frequently.

*   *   *

One consequence of the race relations meetings was that we teachers began to get along better. Not only between races and genders, but between the Sprungs and the Building as well. And in feeling unified, we began to feel emboldened. The SBM meetings had continued and they too helped bring the staff together.

Ms. Jaynes seemed excited about SBM. I suspect this was because Ms. Cornwell was against it. And by the way, I never knew for sure that Cornwell was in fact against it, but she didn't seem as involved to me in getting it off the ground. Much of the time the two women seemed right in step with one another, but often there was a tension between them that you could practically touch. They were both strong women and they had strong views. Though it always seemed to me that Ms. Cornwell was the stronger of the two, Ms. Jaynes was the boss.

There were definitely major differences between the two women. One such difference was that Ms. Jaynes swore which Ms. Cornwell did not approve of. A week or so before my third and final Christmas on Rikers, we had a big Christmas party. We rented a restaurant and spent most of the school day there. This was the result of SBM. Before that, we never had parties that amounted to anything.

In preparing for the day, we had each drawn names and we brought an anonymous Christmas present for the person whose name we had drawn. There were several different rumors concerning who got Ms. Jaynes' name, so it remains a mystery to me. But whoever it was caused a stir.

Ms. Jaynes opened her present in front of everyone. She ripped the wrapping paper off with the abandon of a small child and opened a non-descript box. Inside there was a bunch of gift tissue. She ran her hand through it and pulled out a dildo that was a good ten inches long. She looked at the thing in horror and said, "Who the fuck gave me this?"

Damn, was she ever pissed! When no one admitted to it, she said, "Have some balls and show yourself." Everyone was silent, which made it all the funnier. But no one dared to laugh until later.

Ms. Cornwell took great pride in never using language of that sort. She was a church lady of the highest order. Actually, I think they both were, but apparently in different denominations.

They would have these assemblies for the kids, particularly around Christmas time or Easter, in which several teachers would pray aloud. These were old-fashioned, down home prayers that skirted the edge of speaking in tongues. One of the teachers who prayed in this way was Mr. Maybury— the man whom the kids called Homey the Clown. And it wasn't as if these prayers were prayed simply to the Force of Goodness, or to the Creator or to God. They were addressed to Jesus Christ Almighty who died on Calvary to save us from our sins—let me hear you say "Amen."

I'd look over at Curly and Bill, both of whom were Jewish, and at Mr. Shakir, who was Muslim, and they'd all be smiling at the theater of it. But as far as I know, no one ever complained to the Board of Ed or to the newspaper. I think most of the teachers felt that this was an integral part of Black culture and that maybe it was good for the kids to be exposed to it. Nothing else had worked. Maybe this would.

On the other hand, among our students were members of the Nation of Islam, and many of the kids were Catholic, and that sort of praying was clearly Protestant.

Later, when Mr. Trice showed up and began taking part in these assemblies, the religious aspect of the place got even more intense. Trice, a powerfully built man, would get up there and pray with such fervor that it seemed that by muscle power alone he was determined to get through to God.

He was a bona fide preacher in the African Methodist Church. As far as I know he never had a full time job on Rikers. He was one of several subs who were told to come in every day. Often he would be in the teacher's room when I'd go in there during my prep period and we would talk. He'd try to convert me to Christianity by telling me all about what Jesus had done for him. He'd tell about the days when he was younger and how he would party and have all these women and how he'd been delivered from all of that.

I'd tell him I was glad it was working for him, but that I was incapable of that sort of belief. He was a great guy and I loved talking to him, even when he was trying to proselytize.

Later, a guy by the name of Stephen came along, a young Black man in his twenties, and he too was a serious Christian. He and Trice were clearly working out there primarily to "spread the Word of God."

I don't know what it is about my personality that makes people think they can preach to me. It might be because it's what I'm used to. My mother was like that. She would "witness" to anyone. Our neighbors. The parents of my friends. She'd go to parent teacher conferences and witness to my teachers. And after I left the fold she would witness to me.

Sometimes Stephen would sit with me in the teachers' room and literally preach to me. He'd use his Bible and try to prove to me that the Bible was true. I'd try to explain to him the logical problem of using a thing you're trying to prove as proof, but he didn't seem to get what I was saying. He was an intelligent man, but his faith was blinding.

I'd invariably get more radical and tell him that with language it's impossible to prove anything about the real world. One time I remember telling him about Anselm's Ontological Proof for the Existence of God to help him understand this disconnect between language and the real world.

I told him, "Anselm defined God as 'that being greater than which no being can be conceived.' He said that either that being actually exists, or he exists only in the mind. And since Anselm's definition of God is the greatest being you can conceive of and since, according to Anselm at least, it would be greater if God existed not only in the mind, but in reality as well, then God must exist in reality as well as in the mind."

The thing is, Stephen didn't see the problem with Anselm's logic. He bought it. He thought it was brilliant. He rejoiced that at last someone had actually come up with such a sound argument that proved the existence of God. He asked me to write it down for him. I said, "Sure. But first, I want to use that same argument to show that the greatest possible mile has been run. So, what would the greatest mile be?"

"I don't know," he said. "One that's been run in three minutes?"

"But can't you conceive of a greater mile?"

"Sure."

"Okay, how fast would that mile be?"

"I don't know. One that's been run in no time. In zero seconds."

"Right. So, the greatest mile is that mile faster than which no mile can be conceived. Either that mile has been run in reality or it has been run only in the mind. Since our definition of the greatest mile is the greatest mile you can conceive of, and since it is greater to exist in reality than only in the mind, then that mile must have actually been run. So, a mile that was run in zero seconds has been run."

He laughed and claimed I'd cheated.

*   *   *

It was during my last school year on Rikers that those of us in the Sprungs had a huge Thanksgiving feast for the kids. They knew about our plans in advance and for over a week, they kept bringing it up. I feared they'd be disappointed. Each kid seemed to have a particular dish, without which it would not be Thanksgiving. I couldn't imagine that we would be able to pull off a feast that would meet the expectations of every student.

Several of us cooked turkeys and my memory is that every single teacher in the Sprungs brought in something good to eat. It was an incredible moment. Sometimes as a teacher you look around and suspect that some of your fellow teachers don't care about the kids as much as you do. But on that day, suspicions of that sort faded. As much as it helped the kids to know that we cared about them, I believe it helped each staff member to appreciate the unique contributions of every other member.

That Wednesday morning many of the teachers got there early and we worked together setting up tables in the halls of our respective trailers and arranging the food we'd brought in. Every square inch of those tables was covered with food. I had to carve my turkey at home, of course, because we were not allowed to bring in knives.

That morning, I don't think any of the teachers had the kids do school work. The kids just sat around talking, mostly about what they were going to eat first. During moments like these, they seemed like the most innocent young children imaginable. They told tall tales about how much they had eaten on this or that occasion and they were laughing at anything the way young kids do before they're about to experience something new or unusual. Their innocence was visible.

The doors of most classrooms were open and many of the teachers stood in their doorways talking to each other across the hall. There was a kind of innocent joy among the teachers as well. I think we all felt that we were doing something important. And it wasn't that we didn't feel the teaching we did was important. It's more that after a while it got to be a grind. Under the best of conditions, teachers rarely see that they are making progress. It's certainly different from what it is for, say, carpenters. At the end of the day, a carpenter can see what was accomplished—a staircase was built. A wall was framed. By comparison the temporal increment by which teachers see accomplishment is geologic—especially English teachers. We are fortunate when halfway through the year one of our students can write a well-developed, unified paragraph that makes sense and helps prove a point. On Rikers, everything was so haphazard that observing that sort of progress was rare. But on that day, the difference we were making was right in front of our eyes.

Finally, the time arrived. The kids were brought into the hall one classroom at a time, and we teachers served them. The kids appreciated it in a way that was difficult to predict. I assumed they'd appreciate it. I just didn't expect they would show it. But they did. I don't remember a single kid who didn't express gratitude.

What surprised me most was how polite they were. All of them.

It was amazing how differently they acted when they were treated well. It was enough to make you believe in Maslow's Hierarchy of Needs.

Rumi took a lot of shit for hanging out with me. He was the Malcolm X of RIEF. In his early 30s and angry, he was a poet and writer very much concerned with the Black man's struggle. When he and I started hanging out, it was more than many of his Black friends could comprehend: "One minute he's Brother Malcolm; the next, he's hanging out with Whitey."

I wasn't aware of this at the time, but according to Rumi, after he and I started hanging out, Mr. Rafter, Mr. Stryker, and Danny slowly dialed back their friendship with him.

Rumi believes that these three young men felt as if Rumi had never respected them: after all, they liked sports, and they liked to talk about women and sex, things for which Rumi had little time. While he can be incredibly funny, Rumi is a serious man. He told me he believes those men felt that he considered them frivolous. The thing is, they could not admit any of this to themselves. Instead, he said they simplified the situation in their minds to the point where they saw Rumi as a hypocrite: they said he complained about Whitey, but hung out with Whitey just the same.

One of the things that lends credence to Rumi's view is that before he and I became good friends, I got along with those three guys fairly well. I don't mean that they admitted me to their group. I did, however, have some good talks with each of them one-on-one. During our prep periods, for instance, we'd sometimes discuss music, American history, race in America, religion, our upbringings—all sorts of things. I wasn't aware of it at the time, but looking back on it, all of that slowly ended when Rumi and I started hanging out. After that, while they weren't rude to me, I felt they kept a certain distance.

As that situation was evolving, Mack Paddin joined the faculty. He was an African American man in his twenties whose home room was directly across from mine.

As I've already said, Ms. Cornwell insisted that we teachers write our names, subject areas, aims, and the date on the board as soon as we entered the classroom. In addition, all of us were supposed to have our lesson plans on our desks as we were teaching.

After you figured them out, there really wasn't much to writing aims and lesson plans. Cornwell wanted each aim to be in the form of a question. For instance, "How do I write a four-paragraph essay?" "How do I solve for X in a monomial equation?" "Which compromises helped to maintain the Union during the 1850s?"

Many teachers who ended up on Rikers arrived with zero teaching experience. For the most part, certified teachers did not seek a teaching job out there. Despite the joke that RIEF was the only public school in New York City free of guns, it was a very intense place to teach. That, and getting out there without a car was a nightmare.[12] Keep in mind that fewer than half of NYC households own a car.

If there was an opening, and usually there was, getting a job at RIEF was easy. All you needed was a bachelor's degree and a willingness to become certified. The place was a filtering system such that most teachers who lasted out there were fairly intense. This, of course, increased the likelihood of conflict among faculty members.

Because of my previous teaching experience as an adjunct, in comparison to Mack, I entered Rikers with a fair amount of experience. By the time Mack began, I'd been on the island for over two years. Mack had only been out of college for a couple of years and this was his first teaching gig. He would come across the hall to ask my advice about lesson plans and aims.

Who can explain friendships? On the surface Mack and I had nothing in common. I'm talking less about the obvious differences of age and race than our interests. Mack was a guy who loved to watch sports on television and then argue about these games with friends. He was an all-American male. But somehow we became friends anyway.

Not close friends the way Rumi and I were, but close enough so that one afternoon on his way home from work, he stopped by our loft in Williamsburg. We played pool and drank a couple of beers. My wife came home and joined us. After meeting her, it felt to me that his attitude toward me shifted. I suspect he thought I was rich—why else would such a beautiful woman marry me? And how could we afford to live in a loft in Williamsburg? From then on, he said things that gave me the impression he thought I taught as a hobby.

But still, it felt to me that Mack and I were friends. The trouble was that Rumi's three critics—Mr. Rafter, Mr. Stryker, and Danny—had taken Mack under their collective wing. Mack didn't seem to care about my connection to Rumi. For one thing, at this time Rumi was teaching in the building. No doubt Mack had met Rumi, but I suspect he knew Rumi mainly through his friends' stories about him.

We joked around a lot. I'd make fun of his macho jock-walk. When I'd help him write lesson plans, he'd make references to my White Man's Burden.

Over time, the joking between Mack and me moved from entertaining the two of us to entertaining others. It got to the point that when other teachers were around, Mack and I began pretending for them that we were angry at each other. The people in our trailer knew we were joking. I have no idea how this started or why. It certainly wasn't something we ever decided upon. We just fell into it. It never felt to me that we were actually angry, not even slightly. Instead we were having fun playing the roles of people who are supposed to be angry at each other.

"What the fuck you doing?" I'd ask in an angry sounding voice.

"Chill, old man," he'd say. "I'll get you your meds in a minute."

Later this grew into us physically pushing each other around. One of us would see the other in the hall and pretend to be angry. The other would react in kind. To an outsider, it may have looked as if we were about to fight. For some reason, this seemed like great fun to us.

One Friday morning near the end of the 2nd quarter of my third school year on Rikers, I saw Mack enter the hall while I was standing there talking to Jim. Jim still didn't have his own classroom. Today he was subbing in the Sprungs, but usually The Ladies had him subbing in the building. Because of that, he had never seen Mack and me in action before.

A few days later when I saw Jim, he mentioned the event: "I'm wondering, 'What the fuck is Trask thinking? He's about to get his ass handed to him.' And sure enough, that's what happened. I gotta say, Jay—you had it coming."

I tried to tell him that's what Mack and I always did, but he just said, "You should have told Mack, 'cause he didn't seem to know it."

So, anyway, I stormed over to Mack and said, "Okay, I'm fucking pissed. I'm not taking this bullshit anymore," and I pushed him. This was something we did every day. It was our greeting. On a normal day, if I didn't do it to him, he did it to me.

Rumi later explained to me the dynamics behind Mack's anger. If I had understood those dynamics, I would not have been so stupid. Rumi admits that part of his interpretation is based on speculation. What I do know is that his view of the situation makes the whole thing make sense.

The way he sees it, when Mack's three friends saw Mack and me pushing each other around the hallway day after day, pretending to be on the verge of fighting, they may have begun telling Mack that I was making a fool of him. What's worse, they were probably saying, Mack was allowing it to happen. Rumi suspects they told Mack I was treating him as if he were my "nigger," that I was playing the role of "massa." Rumi's opinion was they had been telling Mack that he, Mack, couldn't see what was going on.

*　　*　　*

Mr. Rafter and Danny had both shown me the ropes when I'd first arrived. They had been extremely generous to me. Then when Mr. Stryker arrived on Rikers, they'd done the same for him.

In fact, for a brief period after Rumi arrived on the scene, Mr. Stryker and I got along fairly well. I think this was before Mr. Rafter and Danny had become his friends. During that period, my son and I went with him and his nieces along with Rumi and his daughter to the Bronx Zoo. We all had a great day together.

I really can't remember when or how things changed between Stryker and me. My memory is that after Mr. Stryker dropped the razor blade, from then on, for reasons I don't understand, things felt strained between us. And I suspect that it was completely separate from the friction between Stryker and Rumi, which I believe resulted from Stryker's growing friendship with Danny and Rafter who had begun to sour on Rumi. But I don't know any of this for sure. All I know for sure is at a certain point, things between Mr. Stryker and me grew complicated.

And things were a bit complicated between Danny and me. Though he eventually seemed to get over it, I had taken his good friend's job.

Between Mr. Rafter and me things were even more complicated. During a prep period, he told me his mother had died when he was quite young. Soon after that, something happened that made her death a complicating factor.

There were no bells announcing the end of periods in the Sprungs, so it was a bit arbitrary as to when one period ended and another began. One day as the period was drawing to a close in my room, two kids began arguing because one of them was claiming loudly that the mother of the other kid was a "ho" back in their neighborhood. He was laughing at the kid and the two of them were on the verge of fighting. The thing kept escalating.

Anxious to avoid a fight, I decided to shock them. I said, "What's the big deal? My mother was a ho." Everyone was suddenly silent and I saw several kids look behind me. That's when I looked around and noticed Mr. Rafter.

Everyone in the classroom was Black except for two Hispanic kids and me. Everyone in the room, including Mr. Rafter looked angry. The fighters were no longer concerned with each other. They were glaring at me.

"Yo, Jay," one of them said. "Why you be dissing your Moms that way?" It was as if I had violated a very ancient code. Well, I guess I had, but, you know…

I said, "It's just language. If I say, 'My mother's a ho,' and she's not, that doesn't make her a ho, right? Right now I'm more concerned that you guys don't fight than I am with whether my mother's a ho."

This started a breakdown of classroom order just as I left. And though I'm sure Mr. Rafter was not thrilled to be left with a group of angry adolescent outlaws, far more disturbing to him was the fact that I'd referred to my mother as a "ho." A few days later, we talked about it in the teachers' room. He spoke in very direct terms against saying those sorts of things to those kids:

"Their mothers are the last thing that's holy to them. And not only that, some of their mothers actually ARE whores. This is not some sort of theory we're talking about. This is the real thing. This is one of the demons some of them are fighting when they go to sleep at night."

All I could say was, "Yeah, well I prevented a fight."

He looked at me as if I were incorrigibly White. He may have had good reason.

So, yeah. Things were complicated with Mr. Rafter as well.

*   *   *

That Friday, as I enter the hall and push Mack and tell him I'm pissed, I have no sense of what may have transpired between Mack and his friends. All I know is that Mack quickly puts me into a bear hug and I put him in a headlock. The difference is that I'm not squeezing hard at all because I believe we're still playing. Mack, on the other hand, starts squeezing so tightly, I fear my ribs are about to pop. I crane my neck to see his face, and what I see gives me pause: he is positively glaring at me. This is no glare of faux anger. This is the real thing. At that moment, he releases one of his arms and grabs my legs and lifts me high into the air. I take another look at him and

I'm horrified. He is pissed. I weigh at least 170 pounds, but he's lifting me as if I weigh 40. At some point, I remember the adage, "What goes up must come down."

It's to keep from being thrown that I squeeze his head more tightly—I have nothing else to hang onto. He, I suspect, interprets my squeezing as me fighting him, and this angers him even more. All I know is I am dreading the landing I predict is in my immediate future.

I'm wondering "Why is he so angry?" I can't make sense of it. I have no idea that Mack's friends may have been filling his head about me. All I know is I am in the middle of a fight, a fight I have zero chance of winning.

Though my fear is that he's picking me up to throw me, I suspect I would have fared better if that's what he'd done. Instead, he raises me to head level and lowers me the way he would a sledge hammer: he slams me into the floor as if to break it.

*   *   *

The fight took place while Guy was in effect running the Sprungs. He was in constant contact with The Ladies. When he carried papers and messages between the Sprungs and the Building, he was consistently being quizzed—on both ends of the trip. In fact, we all suspected he was given this role because Ms. Jaynes knew she could extract information from him. We were forever giving him shit for leaking information to The Ladies.

At some point later that day, when Guy was making his rounds, I picture Ms. Jaynes asking him how things were going out in the Sprungs. Except for the occasional squabble, Guy and I were on fairly good terms. He appreciated the time-saving rides I gave him to the subway station. I suspect he didn't want to tell Ms. Jaynes what had happened between Mack and me.

The thing is, Ms. Jaynes knew how to get to Guy. When I picture the scenario, Ms. Jaynes is simply glaring at Guy as if she knows he has something to tell her. I imagine she does this every time she sees him. Guy fears Ms. Jaynes has already heard. This may be a loyalty test—it wouldn't be the first time she's done that sort of thing. As soon as that thought crosses his mind, Ms. Jaynes smells his fear.

"What are you withholding from me?" I imagine her asking.

"Well," I imagine him answering. "You probably heard about the fight…"

"Of course," comes her shrewd response. "But I want to hear your version. What happened? Tell me the whole thing. I've heard several versions."

"Well," says Guy. "Trask just sort of…I don't know. I wasn't there. But what I heard is he… Well, he just came out of his classroom and started attacking Paddin. So, Paddin got mad and picked Trask up and slammed him to the floor."

"Were students present?"

"No. But a couple of teachers were."

"Who?"

"I don't know for sure. But everyone was talking about it."

"Is Trask all right?"

"Yeah, I guess so."

For all anyone knew, I was all right.

I had been able to protect my head, but I was convinced that my left hip was broken. It turned out that although my hip did bother me for several weeks, it was fine. My right collarbone, on the other hand, was broken.

I got up, looked at Mack and said, "What the fuck?"

I didn't want Mack to know he'd hurt me. I did what I could to hide my limp on my way to my classroom. I sat in the chair closest to the door—a student's chair—and I tried to calm myself. At that moment, I was in such pain I thought I would have to go home. So much adrenaline was coursing through my system I was shivering. I was on the verge of crying—not because of the pain (he hastens to add). It had more to do with feelings of betrayal and confusion.

Maybe three minutes after sitting down, I heard the kids enter the trailer. They always entered with a good deal of fanfare. There was stamping and yelling and pushing. I got up and walked over to my desk and sat on it. When the first student entered the classroom, I greeted him,

"Hey, Jay," he said. He came over and shook my hand. I don't remember who the student was, but I remember talking to him and being in pain and wondering if he could tell. He was clearly too wound up to notice anything.

He started to explain about the visit from the turtles when several other students entered the classroom. At that point I thought we were going to be limited to those four students. A few minutes later, five or six other students appeared. I pulled one of the empty chairs to the front of the class and sat in it. I remember yawning and as I lifted my hand to cover my mouth, that's when I realized my collarbone was broken.

We talked about what had happened to them. "The Turtles" had come in at about two a.m. and had gotten everyone up and terrorized them as they searched for drugs, paraphernalia, and weapons. The students had been up until five. As a result, they didn't feel like doing anything.

On every other occasion this had happened to my students, I felt truly bad as it meant losing class time. But on this occasion, all I could feel was selfish relief that regular teaching today would not work for these kids.

As a result, we spent the next two periods—the homeroom period and period one—talking about what they'd been through and why it had happened. I hoped that neither Ms. Cornwell nor Ms. Jaynes would come over today to check on us. As it turned out, I was lucky. About twenty minutes before our time ended, I handed out paper and asked them to write about what it would feel like to be a Turtle.

I proceeded in a similar manner with all of my classes. Half an hour before my last class of the day ended, Guy knocked on my classroom door and entered.

He told me Ms. Jaynes wanted to see me. He said he would watch my class.

As I walked the quarter mile to the building, I prepared my defense. By the time I got to the elevator, I was nervous that I was about to lose my job.

Ms. Jaynes greeted me in her usual way: "Hello, Trash," she said. She sounded cheerful. She told me she needed me to move to the Building beginning that coming Monday. She said nothing about the fight, so I couldn't bring it up either without looking as if I was attempting to get Mack in trouble.

I told her I would teach in the building if that was my only choice, but that I really loved teaching in the Sprungs.

"Well, of course, you do," she said. "But I really need you to teach over here."

The following Monday, I began my most challenging period of teaching on Rikers.

19. Starting Over

I didn't know it at the time, but I would be teaching on the island for only a few more months.

In the Sprungs, I had grown completely comfortable with my job. I assumed the experience I had gained would be an asset in the Building. I was definitely a little nervous that first day, but I was only nervous the way I always am when I meet a new group of students. If I had known that essentially I was going to have to start from scratch, I would have been far more nervous.

I had no history with the kids. I hadn't proven myself to them. I was just some "herb-ass" White man.

I was given a nice, large classroom right across the hall from Ms. Peterson. When the first kid entered the room, I said, "Hey, what's up?" I told him my name was Jason. He laughed at me.

In the Sprungs, kids would definitely laugh at you. But normally, only if they were in a group. One-on-one, if a kid didn't like you, he might not respond to you, but he wouldn't laugh at you until his friends were there. This kid didn't need a group. He could laugh at me all by himself.

Now, while he didn't *need* an audience, neither did he mind having one. In all, twelve kids entered the room that period. As soon as his friends joined him, he said, "This nigga a corny-ass mother fucker. He be talkin' to me like, 'Hello there. How are you today.'"

I said, "You a lyin' ass mo-fo. That's not what I said. What I said was, 'What's up?'"

"Say word to mother you didn't say, 'Hello there.' Say word to mother."

"Word's bond. You playing yourself. I hope someone's got a shovel. Cause this mother fucker so full of shit we need'ta start shovelin' right now so we don't drown."

The other students are smiling. They're looking back and forth between the two of us. They're not taking my side because I'm new and I'm White. The good news is, they're not taking his side either. In the Sprungs I would have had them laughing by now, but up here in the building they obviously have a better sense of humor. To get them to laugh, it's clear, I'm going to have to work.

The first kid I spoke to is beginning to look amused too, like maybe I have more game than he thought. I ask him his name.

He tells me his name is Elijah. I say, "Well, golly gee. Elijah. Now isn't that a name that originates in the Bible?"

He said, "See what I'm sayin'? That how he be talkin' to me."

I said, "What 'chu talkin' about? How you say I'm talkin'?"

"Like you just did. 'Golly gee' and shit.

I said, "Yo, man. Are you for real? I didn't say that. Did any'a you hear me say 'Golly gee'?"

One kid said, "No," and he was grinning big and then another kid agreed and Elijah started going nuts.

He said, "Oh, so it like that, ha?" He was grinning now.

I asked them their names and they all told me, though one kid claimed his name was "Nun-ya."

I said, "Oh, Nunya. What a nice name. Let me guess. Is your last name 'Business'?"

He looked annoyed and put his head on his desk. The rest of us talked for a while about what they'd been doing in English before I came. They were pissed off because their English teacher before me was Ms. Davis, an exceptionally nice Black woman whom I knew and respected. And here I was, neither Black nor woman. They didn't seem to hold it against me. They held it against Ms. Jaynes for moving Ms. Davis to the other hall.

At some point during that first class, a female correction officer walked past our door. One of the kids said, "Yo, Mister. Get that CO in here. She lookin' for me."

I stepped into the hall and called to her. "Ma'am?" There weren't a lot of women COs out there, but she was definitely the prettiest one I had seen. I told her a student in my room was claiming she was looking for him.

She smiled as if she knew what was up but she came over to the door and stepped in. The kid who'd called for her had his hands in his pants and he was overtly jerking off right there. When I saw what was going on I said to him, "Man, you really know what's up with women." I apologized to the CO and she left, all smiles. This had apparently happened to her before.

The kid said, "Why you be tellin' her to go. You's a dumb mother fuck-er."

"You're catchin' money in front of a woman you don't even know, and I'm the dumb mother fucker? You're killin' me, bro."

"Where you hear that at?" one of the kids asked.

"Hear what?"

"Catchin' money."[13]

"I've been teaching in the Sprungs until now," I said, "and that's where I heard it."

"Why you be coming over here now?" one of them asked.

"Good question. I don't really know. Ms. Jaynes told me to."

"Niggas in the Sprungs got you under pressure?"

"Yeah, just like you guys got me under pressure. I don't know why they sent me here. I liked it out there, but it looks like it'll be okay here too. I don't much care."

"How long you be out there for?"

"Nearly two and a half years."

"Which trailer you in?"

"The third one."

"Who be teachin' there?"

"Mr. Scott, Dr. Steele, Mr. Paddin, Mr. Cumberbatch, Mr. Malcore. Why? Did you spend some time out there?"

"Yeah, but before you came. When I was there Mr. H was there."

"Yeah," I said. "I heard he was a nice guy. I took his place, actually, after he left."

"Mr. H, he a good teacher."

"That's what I've heard."

When that first class ended, though I felt relieved, I believe that was the first moment I considered leaving Rikers.

Most of the classes had under fifteen students except the one in Ms. Peterson's room. She had about twenty-five kids and going in there seemed like hell after a while. But on the first day I didn't have any problems.

It was always like that out there. As long as you didn't try to get anything done other than get to know the kids, things went smoothly. But as soon as you began to put pressure on them to do some work, it got difficult. They were in jail. They were worried about what was going to happen in court. They were worried about what was going on at home with their friends and families. Expecting them to do school work under those conditions, was asking a lot. I could barely get myself to do school work when I was their age and I wasn't even in jail.

I spent the first class focusing on getting to know them and just talking to them about things that mattered to them and I let them ask me questions about my personal life. They all wanted to know if I was married, if I had kids, how old they were, where I grew up, if I lived in Bensonhurst, if I ate "the pussy," if I'd ever had sex with a Black woman.

Another question they asked me was the one about if someone offered me a million dollars to kill someone and I knew I wouldn't get caught, would I do it.

By now I'd come to realize that this was the question many Rikers kids asked adults to see if they could trust them. If the adult answered, "No," then the adult was clearly a liar. The thought that someone would not kill for a million dollars on principle was unthinkable to most of them, given the people they had encountered and the bits and pieces of news they had heard about politicians and the rich and famous.

I asked them how many of them would do it. Every kid in the class raised his hand. I said, "I realize that in asking that question, you're trying to find out if I'm a bullshitter. Kids in the Sprungs asked me that same question. The thing is, I believe if I'd grown up like some of you may have grown up—and I don't actually know how any of you as individuals grew up, but I know how many of the kids in the Sprungs told me they grew up—and if I had grown up like that, I suspect I'd kill for a million dollars too. But I've got to tell you, if you were to ever meet my father, I think you'd believe me when I say that I wouldn't kill for a million dollars. When he was twelve years old, he bought a .22 for something like twelve dollars from Sears and Roebuck."

"Twelve dollars for a .22?" a kid named Tyson said. "Your father be telling some stories."

The kids all laughed.

"No, seriously," I said. "Twelve dollars. He still has it. I've shot it."

"Okay," he said. "Then, you telling stories. Didn't no one buy no .22 for no twelve dollars."

"Sure he did. You guys ever heard of inflation? Anyone?"

"Yeah," said a kid named Brunel. "That's when your money isn't worth anything."

"Yeah, basically. When there's inflation, money becomes worth less and less over time. So it takes more money over time to get ahead. And when my father was a kid you could buy a loaf of bread for like twenty-five cents and a simple house for a couple thousand dollars. And you could buy a brand-new, single-shot .22 for twelve dollars. It's actually a very nice gun. It's a bolt action, single-shot .22. At any rate, when he got it…"

"Where'd he get the money at?" Brunel said.

"He had a paper route. He'd delivered papers to people every morning before school. He probably didn't even make a dollar a week doing that, but he saved his money and bought the rifle. He's always been like that. I can't save money, but he's always been good at it. So like I was saying, when he got the thing, he took it out in the woods near where he lived…"

"Where he be living at?" said Tyson.

"East Wilton, Maine."

"East Wilton, Maine? They be fucking pigs out in there, right?"

"Why," I asked. "You looking for a place like that?"

Everyone laughed, Tyson too.

"I'm sayin'," he said.

"What are you saying? Are you saying yes?"

They laughed some more. "Anyway, so he was out there in the woods and he saw a squirrel and he shot it. And when he saw the squirrel's body, he sat down on a tree stump and cried and vowed never to kill another thing in his life."

"He a herb," someone said.

"Well, maybe," I said. "But he was also a war hero."

"Wait a second," said Brunel. "I thought you said he didn't kill."

"That's just it. It was something that bothered him even though he personally never did any killing."

"Well, if he didn't kill, how was he a war hero?"

"He was in the Air Force—well, actually, the Army Air Corps. He was awarded two Air Medals and the Distinguished Flying Cross. He was a navigator on a B-29, the largest airplane that existed back in World War Two. It was a bomber. But he didn't drop the bombs. He was the plane's navigator. That's the guy who figures out how to get the plane to where the bombs need to be dropped. And he always felt ambivalent about it. You guys know that word? Ambivalent?"

"Yeah," said Brunel. "That's how I feel while I'm fucking your wife."

"Oh," I said, remembering my line from the Sprungs: "So you're that guy? She's been talking in her sleep about some guy with a little dick."

Everyone laughed and Brunel smiled. He didn't have a comeback the way Tony had.

"Anyway," I continued. "In terms of killing, my father made an exception for insects and fish, but even with those two species, he would often catch them and let them go. And he brought me up to think that life—all life— is precious. It's really the only thing that's worth anything, when you think about it. You know? Cause when you die, it's not as if you can take your possessions with you."

"You can't take your life with you either."

"That's true."

"So how's life different?"

"That's a great question, Brunel. I think life is different because it's what makes everything else possible—at least temporarily. Without life you couldn't do anything, you couldn't have anything, you couldn't know anything, you couldn't feel anything, you couldn't experience anything. What else is there that's like that? A million dollars isn't like that. If you've got a million dollars but you don't have life, there's no you to spend it. But if you've got life without a million dollars, a lot can happen. You don't need a million dollars, but you need your life."

"Yeah, but if you've got life, you can experience bad things too."

"That's true."

"So what's so great about life?"

"Another good question, and ultimately, I guess I don't have a good answer for it. But at least if you have life, you have the potential, the possibility to experience good things."

"What if someone give to you a million dollars if you kill some homeless man," said Tyson.

"No. I couldn't live with myself. I would feel terrible for the rest of my life that I had taken the only thing the man had, his life, and that I had done it so that I could be living large."

"What's wrong with living large?" said Brunel.

"Nothing, but I don't want to do it at the expense of another person. And just think about his relatives. I don't want to steal this man from his relatives."

"What if he was homeless and didn't have relatives?"

"I wouldn't do it."

"What if he was a killer?"

"No."

"Now you're bullshitting," said Brunel.

"I don't even believe in capital punishment."

"Okay," said Tyson. "What if he a killer and homeless and he don't got relatives and he gonna die in ten minutes anyway."

"No."

"Man, you a freak," he said.

"And a liar," added another kid.

I said, "Do you think killing is right? Do you honestly believe killing is right? And I'm not talking about if you're the one doing the killing. Do you want people running around killing each other whenever they feel like it?"

Some of them thought they did. I asked how many of them either had kids or wanted to have kids. They all raised their hands. I said, "Imagine you've got a baby daughter, and someone comes around and kills her for a million dollars. How are you going to feel?"

Tyson said, "I'm gonna feel like bustin' a cap in that mother fucker's ass. But first I'm gonna bust a cap in his hands, in his arms, in his feet, his ankles, his shins, his dick, and I'm gonna leave him like that so he suffers. And then after he passes out, I'm gonna wake his ass up and kill his sorry self. Don't no one be killing my baby daughter."

"Exactly. And do you want to live in a world in which people are going around and killing each other like that?"

I went into my Thomas Hobbes spiel about without the social contract life would be 'nasty, short and brutish.'

"You want to live like that?" I asked. "If you had a choice, wouldn't you rather have everyone having all the shit they need and no one is killing anyone else for their shit?"

They thought about it for a while. Brunel laughed and said he'd like to have everyone else be peaceful and for him to be the only criminal. That idea was one they all went for.

"So," I said. "It looks like you wouldn't be the only one for long. All of your classmates would join you. And other people are going to have the same idea. If you want to live in a better world, then you have to stop doing that shit and have faith that other people are going to stop."

They told me that life wasn't ever going to be like that on this earth. I agreed that there would always be crime, but the fewer people who did it, the better, and every time one person stops, that makes things a little better. And the only person that I could really stop from doing crime was myself. And if I do that, then my kids will know and hopefully they won't do crime either.

"What about smoking buddha?" Brunel asked.

"What about it?"

"Is smoking buddha a crime?"

"It is right now, but I don't think it should be."

"So you think weed should be legalized?"

"Definitely."

"Why?" said Tyson. "You be smoking that shit, right?"

"I think it should be legalized because it doesn't work to make it illegal. It didn't work to make alcohol illegal either when they had the prohibition. How many of you are in here because of selling weed?"

Four of them raised their hands.

"How many of you who are here on weed never stuck anyone up or committed a violent crime?"

One kid raised his hand. When he saw he was the only one, he lowered it and looked embarrassed. One of the other kids said to him, "You a herb," and two other kids repeated it.

I said, "How's he a herb? He's never stuck a kid up. How's that being a herb?"

Without having to stop to think about it a kid said, "Cause if he don't stick people up, then other people be stickin' him up."

I said, "I don't follow your logic. What do you mean?"

Tyson explained it: "There ain't but two types of niggas. Niggas who be robbin' and niggas who be getting robbed."

"What do you mean," I asked. "I've never robbed anyone and I've never been robbed."

"Yeah, but you don't be livin' where we live."

"I live in Williamsburg. I've met kids in here from Williamsburg."

"Where you live in Williamsburg."

I told him.

"People don't be robbin' people up in there where you be living. South of Metropolitan down toward the bridge, down there niggas be robbin' niggas. Go down there in about three more months, and I'll hook you up."

We all laughed.

I wanted clarification. "So you mean to tell me that where you come from, everyone either robs or gets robbed."

They all agreed—that's how it was. Then one of them added, "Some be doin' both."

At the time I thought their ideas about killing people for a million dollars had to do with where they'd grown up and the fact that they didn't have caring parents. What amazed me more was what happened after I began teaching in a small town high school in Maine. One day a group of honors freshmen asked me what teaching on Rikers had been like. As I told them about it, I mentioned being asked the question: "If you were promised a million dollars for killing someone and you knew you wouldn't get caught, would you do it?" The honors kids asked me, "What did you say?"

"What do you mean what did I say?" I was completely amazed that they would even ask the question. "I said no."

I could see from their faces that they were surprised. It then occurred to me to ask the question of them: "How many of you would kill for a million dollars?"

One of them asked, "And I wouldn't get caught?"

"Right," I said. "You wouldn't get caught."

Nearly all of the kids in the class raised their hands. It didn't seem possible to me. Here they were middle class kids. They'd all grown up in relative comfort and most of them had two parents.

I said to them, "Are you kidding me? You would actually take another person's life just so you could have a million dollars?"

One of them said, "A million dollars is a lot of money."

Later that the year I had those same kids write persuasive essays about capital punishment. Nearly all of them were in favor of it. I said, "But what about the fact that you said you would kill for a million dollars?"

One young woman justified it with, "But you said we wouldn't get caught."

Since then, I've asked that question to a number of classes with similar results.

Apparently kids these days have seen through the veneer behind which we've been hiding our true values. We're like an accountant with two sets of books. In one of them we keep the values we preach; in the other, the values we actually live by. Kids are definitely paying attention to that latter set.

20. Building Teachers

Curly was one of the funniest guys I've ever met anywhere. He had been working on Rikers for over twenty years and he had seen it all. Originally, he'd been a classroom teacher, but somehow he had found his way into Ms. Cornwell's good graces and now he was, in effect, her footman. He hung around the office, and when she or the secretary had an errand to be run, he would take care of it. Many of those who had been there for a long time considered this a tragedy since the word was that he had been an incredibly effective teacher.

What was clear to us all is that he had terrific one-upsmanship skills. He came out on top in every exchange. In the battle of the wits there was no besting him.

Sometimes he would walk past a classroom and the kids would call out to him, "Yo, Curly. Come talk to us." He would stick his head in the door and the kids would begin asking questions to hear his Don Rickles type responses.

"Hey, Curly. What 'chu doin' tonight?"

"Whadaya think I'm doing?" he'd say. "I'm gonna go sell crack to your Mama just like I always do."

Everyone would laugh.

"Where she be at?" another kid would say.

"Stop with the stupid questions. She's selling herself down on Forty-Ninth and Tenth just like she always does."

"You gonna get some of that pussy for yourself?"

"The price is right, that's for sure. Thing is, I'm afraid she'll give me another dose of the clap."

The degree to which his responses were shocking was the degree to which the kids laughed. In more than a few cases what he said probably hit close to home with someone in the room.

It made me wonder what he was doing that was different from what I had done that day the kids got so upset with me. One day it hit me: he was not calling his own mother a 'ho' the way I had. He was calling their mothers ho's. You would assume that the kids would be upset about it, but I never saw a kid show any anger or resentment toward Curly. That's probably because the only kids who asked him questions were the ones who could deal with his answers.

*   *   *

Jim was finally given his own classroom in the building. He was an English teacher. He'd substituted at a number of schools, most of which were in Queens, where he'd grown up. He told of teachers who sat at their desks all day reading the newspaper. In some cases they were too afraid to do anything else; in others they made an agreement with the kids:

"I don't want trouble. You don't want trouble. You don't bother me; I won't bother you. Do you follow me?"

Jim was one of the most gifted English teachers I've ever seen. He had a way of getting his students interested in all sorts of literature, including complicated poetry. He would ask them a series of Socratic questions through which he drew them to an interpretation. Once I remember he did a lesson on Shelley's sonnet, "Ozymandias."

When he told me he intended to teach it, I remember wondering how he was ever going to accomplish it. But he got the kids interested in taking it apart. He got them to see the poem as having been written in a sort of code. And since the kids spoke in a code, they loved the idea of breaking someone else's.

At some point, the two of us started sitting in my classroom where we'd smoke cigarettes during our lunch break. This of course was verboten. The DOC didn't care if we smoked. COs smoked all over the place. But since smoking is not allowed in public schools anywhere in America, Jaynes and Cornwell didn't want us smoking. Curly seemed to be immune from that rule, as were a few others. Jim and I hadn't been teaching there long enough.

The problem was that each of the classrooms in the building had a small window cut into the wall through which the COs could observe.

I had moved my desk to the side of the room and it happened to be right in front of that small window and I sat with my back to it. One day when Jim and I were sitting there talking about nearly everything, he said something that reminded me of the song made famous by the Trashmen, "Surfin' Bird," the song that's sometimes called "Bird Is the Word."

I begin singing it, really getting into it and I'm belting it out over and over, getting louder each time through. Jim is laughing at me and suddenly the look on his face changes and I see him looking over my head. I turn around and there stands Ms. Cornwell looking in at us through the little window, wondering, apparently, about the source of the noise.

Up until that moment it always felt to me as if she had thought of me as a harmless White boy, but that she now realized there was more to the picture. The good news was that even though she'd seen Jim's cigarette, I was fairly certain she hadn't seen mine: I was too close to the window. She walked over to the door and said to him, "Is that a cigarette I saw in your hand?"

He said, "Yes, it is."

"Please do not smoke in the classrooms. If you need to smoke, you know where you can do so, is that not true?"

"Yes, it is, Ms. Cornwell."

"Thank you."

She now looked at me. By now I had successfully cuffed my cigarette and I was sitting there looking at her. She smiled at me and said, "I didn't realize you were a singer, Mr. Trask."

I said, "Well, normally I keep it on the D.L."

She shook her head and smiled. Just before leaving she said, "By the way, Mr. Trask. I trust you heard what I said about smoking."

I said, "Absolutely," and she left.

That was Ms. Cornwell. As long as you knew your place, she was fine.

* * *

Most of the people who lasted on Rikers had overtly strong personalities. There were some, however, who didn't wear their strength on their sleeves. I'd meet them and think, "They won't last a week out here." But a year later they'd still be there. One such man was Mr. Pittman.

Pittman was a retired IBM executive. My first impression of him was that being Black was something he would rather not acknowledge. I thought of him as White through and through. Later I realized that the way I pegged him was evidence of my own racial prejudice, not his. I had an idea of what a Black man should be. I had met hundreds of Black men by that point in my life and in my arrogance, I thought I had an idea of what it meant to be Black.

At any rate, I felt that Pittman was definitely a wanna-be White guy. He probably thought of me as wanna-be Black. If that is so, he was no doubt closer in his estimation of me than I was in mine of him.

He was about five eight and in fairly good shape. In my memory he always wore a White shirt and a tie. He wore gold rimmed glasses that gave him a meticulous look. If that wasn't enough, his close-cropped mustache did the trick. To tell you the truth, I don't remember if he had a mustache or not, but in my memory he does. He stood erect and my first impression of him was that he was extremely exacting. He was precise in his movements and manner, but not effeminate. I guess the word for him is "gentleman."

Now Dr. Steele was a gentleman as well, and I've obviously known other Black gentlemen. But Steele came closer to fitting my idea of a strong Black man. Now, it wasn't that Pittman appeared weak. It's more that he was one of those men who didn't feel the need to prove anything, and that's about as strong as it gets.

The more I got to know Mr. Pittman, the more I grew to admire him. It was not difficult to see that he had done well at IBM. He had no reason to work, and he especially had no reason to do such stressful work. Clearly he was trying to give something back to his community.

In effect, Pittman was volunteering out there and the Black kids in his classes gave him a far harder time than they gave many of us. At least in the beginning. The kids suffered from the same mischaracterization of him I had. But in the end they came around and respected him. Again, as long as you were yourself, you were fine out there.

21. Building Students

It took me a while to get used to teaching in the building, and I never got to be as comfortable over there as I had been in the Sprungs. For one thing, I wasn't there for as long.

Jim and I were both English teachers for the same four classes of students. The way I recall it, he focused primarily on literature and I focused on writing. Once again I had four groups of kids to teach, including my homeroom kids whom I had for two periods.

My homeroom, it turned out, was a fairly easy group to deal with after I got to know them. The next room down was less predictable. I'd go in there and not know what to expect. There was a kid in there by the name of Jason who would sit with his head on his desk every day, apparently sleeping. The only time he would sit up was to answer a question. And his answer was always the same. If I said to the class, "Okay, so say you're taking the GED writing exam: what's the first thing you think about before you begin answering the question?"

Jason would sit up looking drowsy and yell loudly, "My dick." Then he'd chuckle to himself and put his head back on his desk. Or a kid would ask me, "Yo, why you be teachin' out here?"

Jason would answer, "My dick."

But Jason wasn't an actual problem. After all, he was usually asleep. The problem was this kid who wouldn't stop talking. He kept a running commentary during the entire period. He was very funny and a very likeable kid.

And then came the day when he interrupted a class discussion, and out of nowhere said to me, "When I get up out of here, I'm gonna find you and I'm gonna slide up inside you."

This was yet another moment you're not told about in education classes. A couple of ideas ran through my head about how to respond, but no ideas could compete with the adrenaline that was surging through me.

I charged over to him, looked him directly in the eye, and I shoved my hand up to his throat and squeezed. I said, "Don't you ever say that to me again." After that, I returned to the front of the room and tried to remember what I'd been saying.

That is definitely one of the moments out there I wish I could redo. The truth is, no one had ever threatened to rape me before and I have to say, it scared me. And the thing that scared me most was that he and the other students would see that it scared me. Rikers was not the sort of place where you wanted your students to see your fear.

*   *   *

Across the hall from there was a kid by the name of Michael. Like Tony, Michael was one of my all-time favorite students. He was one of the most intelligent, most personable kids I've ever met. And he had one of the most incredibly philosophical and curious natures you're likely to find among teenagers. He was open to anyone who had something to teach him. And I'm convinced that this was not just a matter of public relations. He truly wanted to learn how to write better. He wanted to know how to read better. He wanted to understand the things he read. He wanted to hear how the political system worked. He wanted to understand why White people are the way we are.

He would ask direct questions about the behavior of White people and he would honestly be trying to understand what made us tick, trying to understand why we are so strange. And he did all of this in a completely polite and respectful way.

I met a lot of kids there about whom I thought, "If someone could just adopt this kid and bring him home everything would be fine for him." Even after I found out what Michael had done I didn't change my mind about him being a great kid. He told me he'd begun selling drugs because he wanted nice things. It was just his mother and he at home, and she couldn't afford the sorts of things he felt he deserved. He admitted it was selfish and inconsiderate of him to feel that way, but that's how he'd felt. He said he began selling drugs when he heard how much money kids were making.

A guy had fronted him the drugs and had expected him to sell them and pay him back. They would share some of the profit, but he, Michael wouldn't see as much as he would have if he had bought the drugs up front. He was something of a sharecropper—in fact, this was true of many of my students.

At any rate, someone came up to him one day and robbed him of his money, including the money he owed to his supplier. Michael was scared. He had to get that money back or he feared he was dead. These guys didn't mess around. His guy would think Michael was playing him if he didn't come up with that money. He told me he'd gone after the kid who robbed him.

After I left the island, a friend who worked there told me some of the details that Michael had left out. He had shot at the kid who'd stolen the money from him, but he had missed and the bullet killed a young boy.

One day we had an open house to which parents were invited to talk to us about their sons' educational progress. It took all sorts of coordination on the part of the school and the jail to make it happen, but it was potentially very useful. It was one of the times that Jaynes and Cornwell came through in a huge way.

I met five of my students' parents—all of them mothers—and Michael's mom was among them. She was a very striking woman who appeared well educated. But the thing she seemed most concerned about was letting us know that she had not raised Michael to end up in jail. I told her it was clear that Michael was a lot more than a mere criminal.

From what I heard, Michael was given a fairly long sentence. I hope he was not destroyed by his stay in prison. He was an incredibly gifted young man and if a couple of variables had played out differently in his life, I suspect he would have been hugely successful. He may be yet. It wouldn't surprise me at all to hear that he had left his past behind.

*   *   *

I hadn't been in the building very long when I started having problems with the students in Ms. Peterson's room, which as I said, had more students than the other rooms I taught in. I began to dread going in there. It felt like they had my number. The GED was coming up. One day I found a practice GED essay question about whether we should ban cigarettes and went in there and attempted to teach them how to structure the GED essay.

There was this student making all sorts of noise over by the window and I went over to him and put my hand on his desk and leaned over and asked him to quiet down. The situation was nearly identical to the one in which Machete "stabbed" my hand with the pencil.

I was purposely kind of getting in this kid's face because I knew he was trying to intimidate me and I wanted to show him and everyone else that it wouldn't work. He was looking at a specific spot on my face as if there were something there that I needed to wipe off, a standard Rikers intimidation technique. It makes you feel as if you should put your hand to that spot to see if there's something there. But if you do it, you signal to the kid that he has made you lose your confidence. Not only that, by looking at you this way, he can avoid looking you in the eye, avoid human contact with you. That way, he has more options, i.e., he doesn't have to worry about his pesky conscience.

I let him look and I fought the urge to feel for a stray booger. We just kept looking at each other for half a minute or so. Everyone in the classroom was silent.

He finally said, "Get your hands off my desk or I'll stick this pencil in your eye."

My body wanted to pull back immediately. But I had gotten to know this kid a bit and I liked him. I didn't think he would do it. I pulled my head closer to him and said, "Why's that? So I'll be as ugly as you?"

He began laughing and everyone else did too. He then said the most unexpected thing I ever heard out there: "Yo, Jay. You got them mad social skills." At that point I laughed too.

After that things got back on track for a few minutes until a new student who was sitting in the middle of the classroom said to me, "Why you be teaching us this bullshit?"

I said, "What bullshit is that?"

"About banning cigarettes. They ain't gonna ban no cigarettes."

"I agree with you."

"Then why you teaching us about it?"

I said, "I'm not teaching you about banning cigarettes. I'm teaching you how to write an essay."

"You not teaching us about banning cigarettes? Then why you keep talking about banning cigarettes?"

"Well, I'm trying to teach you guys how to write an essay so you can pass the GED test. In order to do that, you have to practice, and we're just practicing right now. We could be writing this about anything. We could be writing about abortion, you know? About capital punishment. About anything. About whether to legalize marijuana, whether there should be a draft, or whatever. Anything you might have an opinion about we can practice writing about."

"The only thing I have an opinion about is this is bullshit. You be teaching niggas all this stuff that ain't never gonna happen. They ain't never going to ban no cigarettes."

"But like I said, I'm not trying to teach that they will ban cigarettes."

"No? Then why you be talking about banning cigarettes all the time? Look what it say on the board? Do it say all kind of shit about banning cigarettes or not?"

"Yes it does, but…"

"That's right, and that's cause you be teaching us about banning cigarettes and then you act like you not. That's that bullshit. You's a dumb mother fucker. Think a nigga don't know what you teaching?" By now it was fairly clear that he knew the deal and was just messing with me.

No matter what I said to him he wouldn't shut up. At one point he tried to get me to come over to him and he would show me something I could teach. "Do like you done with that other kid," he said. "Put your face up in mine like you done with him."

I wanted to say something to get the other kids laughing, but my instincts told me not to mess with him and to stay away from him. He was angry at me in a highly unusual way. I didn't know him—it was the first time he'd been in my classroom. Moreover, he had a long, fresh red scar across his face. You could see where the stitches had recently been removed, and he was becoming increasingly agitated.

I finally opened the door and asked Marvin, the CO, to talk to him, something I only did a couple of times while I was on the island. He came and pulled the student out, literally. He later told me he searched the kid and found a razor. The kid was put in the Bing. After that, I never saw him again. I don't know what happened to him, but I hope things worked out well for him.

When I told other teachers about it, they all doubted that he would have used the razor on me. But I didn't doubt it for a minute, nor do I doubt it now. Something was going on with that kid that day. On the other hand, during the three school years I was on Rikers I never heard of a teacher being cut, though a couple of teachers were hit by students. But it always seemed to me that the possibility of being cut existed in a real way, especially if you had a certain type of annoying personality, which I definitely have.

Later, when there were only about twelve students in that classroom, I got quite close to the group who remained. One day I was in the back of the room reading some poems to them. I don't know why, but when I entered the classroom that day, all of the desks had been pushed against the back wall of the classroom so that together they formed a kind of square.

Whatever the reason, the kids and I ended up sitting on those desks. I was sitting cross-legged and leaning against the wall as I read the poems to them. The students were gathered around me and really seemed to be listening. Out of the corner of my eye I noticed one of them get up and walk over to the door, which he opened and scanned the hall. I looked up and saw him nod to a kid who was sitting beside me. I realized that they were either *pretending* to set up to cut me, or they were *actually* setting up to cut me.

A jolt of fear buzzed through me. But I kept reading and I thought about how all of these kids in the room liked me. It was palpable every day I was in there. We all got along with each other. I decided they were messing with me—but I didn't know for sure.

Peripherally, I am aware of the kid beside me getting up on his knees—we are still sitting on the desks. I can see him reach around behind himself and stick his hand in his sagging pants as if "pulling out on me."

He reaches in now and out of the corner of my eye I see him put his hand up to his mouth as if he's biting off the plastic to expose the corner of the blade—or at least that's what he's trying to make me think.

I continue to read and I pretend not to notice. Part of me is definitely nervous, but I'm thinking there is no way this kid has anything against me. I'm convinced—well, nearly convinced—that these guys are messing with me, that they want to see how I'll react and whether I'll lose my shit.

I'm also thinking, "What if I'm wrong."

"But I'm not," I tell myself.

"But what if I am?"

I finally decide that the worst that can happen is that I'll have a scar across my face that I'll probably be able to have fixed, and even if I can't, it's not going to kill me and it will always give me a good excuse to tell a story about my time teaching on Rikers. The only thing that gives me pause is the way they're all in on it. But then I realize that's exactly why I can feel safe: I know that as a group these kids like me. There is no way they would all be in on it.

I keep reading. And then I see the kid move his hand through space and it's coming toward me. I continue to read and I'm certain I'm correct, and his hand comes down across my face and I know from talking to the kids that it doesn't hurt at first when you get cut with a razor, and this doesn't hurt, so I still don't know if it's real or not. They watch me for about five seconds and when I keep reading, they all burst out laughing. One of them says, "See, I told you."

Another kid said, "Was you scared, Jay?"

I smiled. "Scared of what?" They all laughed.

So then they all wanted to know if I had noticed the kid over by the door. I said I had. They just kept asking me why I didn't try to defend myself and I said, "Cause I knew you guys don't have beef with me."

The kid with the fake blade showed me what he had. He had folded a piece of paper and into the shape of a Bic blade, and wrapped it in plastic from a cigarette pack.

For the next few days they argued over whether I'd been afraid. The truth is, even though I was ninety-nine percent certain nothing was going to happen, I was still scared. But I was extremely glad I hadn't reacted.

I never did tell them the real reason I hadn't reacted. It was because of Michael. He was one of my best friends after we moved to Maine from Massachusetts when I was eleven. He was a guy who played tricks on people constantly. One of these tricks involved scaring you, making you jump or show some sort of reaction. For instance he'd raise his hand as if he intended to hit you, and then when you'd react, he'd scratch his head and look at you as if, "What's wrong with you?" He did this sort of thing to everyone. It was constant with him and if you reacted in the smallest way, he would laugh until he was wheezing. He was the best trainer a person could have for teaching in a place like Rikers.

22. Ham

The summer after my third school year on Rikers, my family and I moved to a small town in Maine where I got a job teaching high school English. We moved for a number of reasons, the primary one of which was financial. My wife was pregnant and did not want to work outside the home after our baby was born.

As a result, we could no longer afford to live in New York City. Living there on a teacher's salary with three kids is impossible. What's ironic is that in moving to Maine, we got by on about half of what our combined salaries in New York City had been.

Along with Vermont and New Hampshire, Maine is among the whitest states in the country. And while it is a blue state, there is a lot of ignorance on display here with regard to race. For instance, I have heard people who otherwise strike me as liberal or progressive, refer to African Americans as "colored." It's as if no one ever told them there is a problem with that term.

New Yorkers are not like that. Not overtly.

New York sees itself as this bastion of liberalism, the antithesis of racism. Yet there's still a kind of hostility on the part of White people toward Black people that's undeniable. And, sure, it goes the other way too. But, hey— given the history of race relations in this country, I feel that the making-things-right ball is in the White people's court.

Many of my White friends appear embarrassed for me when I make statements of that sort. Actually, some of my Black friends do as well. They see it as patronizing. I don't much care. That's how I see it.

If you're comparing apples to apples—that is, White people and Black people who are on an equal socio-economic footing—just about all White people have advantages in this society that just about no Black people have.[14] How can you deny that?

If everyone in this country were equal, it would be considerably more difficult for White people to get a job or an apartment, a loan from a bank, etc., than it currently is. All of that is just part of White Privilege.

These days when I visit New York I see signs that things have *begun* to change. But even now, romantic involvement between Blacks and Whites is way ahead of close friendships between those same two groups. The romantic involvement definitely bodes well for the future. But it's only a beginning.

When I lived in New York, it's true that Blacks of good will and Whites of good will got along with each other, and were definitely friendly. But more often than not, those friendships were superficial, that is, the friendships did not transcend the social setting within which they were formed. If friends met at work, that's where the friendship stayed.

In my experience, the norm among New Yorkers of both races is that they are hard-nosed. One night a Black friend was visiting me in my apartment. We were drinking beer and talking when a White friend stopped by. While they were getting to know each other, the White guy brought up a controversial Black leader as if the man were a joke, and that was it. The two of them got into a fairly nasty argument. I sat there cringing. After the argument had gone on for a while, my Black friend left and he did not seem pleased.

At that point, I mentioned to my White friend that he could have maybe taken it a little easier on my other friend. Why, he wanted to know. I brought up the fact that he might have felt as if it was two White guys ganging up on a Black guy. He said I was being ridiculous. In fact, if anyone should have been threatened it was he because several times I had interjected my opinion and had come down on the side of the Black guy. Then he said, "You grew up in Maine. What do you know about Black people?"

The White guy maintained that he had acted the same way he would have acted if he had been in an argument with a White guy. And knowing him, I do believe that's true. For him that was the absence of racism. But I think something else needs to happen. To him, my view is condescending.

If I'm trying to get my friendship back on track with another person whom I've wronged, the next time I see that other person, I'm careful not to do or say anything that could be misinterpreted as me not caring. White people have enslaved, lynched, and disenfranchised Black people for 400 years. Our record of friendship toward Black people is suspect. White people have only been attempting to turn things around for 50 years or so, and even that has been half-hearted. That's the equivalent of being acquainted with a person for eight years and screwing him over for seven of those years and half screwing him over for one of those years. Under those circumstances, chances are your friend will feel some suspicion.

I always visit Rumi when I go to New York. I finally got him to come visit me up here in Maine, but it took some doing. Like I said, Maine is among the Whitest states in the nation. When I first suggested the visit, he was reluctant. I guess he had good reason to be. He remembered when I was living in Williamsburg, and I kept telling him how open that section of Brooklyn was, that I saw no evidence of racism.

He sometimes rode to work with me in the morning. On one such day, we stopped at a deli near my house. I ordered first. The woman was sweet to me just as she always was. Then Rumi ordered. He was wearing a kufi hat, a Muslim-looking affair, and he ordered a croissant with butter. The woman asked impatiently, "Ham?"

Rumi was confused. He stood there trying to decide what she meant and she said again, "Ham?"

"No," Rumi said. "Just butter."

"With ham?" the woman asked insistently.

"No. Just butter."

Unbelievably she repeated it again. "Ham?"

It was clearly her way of making sure he would never return to her shop. She thought he was Muslim and she was making him uncomfortable by bringing up ham. Yet she did it in a way that, to other customers, it would not appear racist.

Another time I went with him to a department store. Since my mid-twenties I don't recall ever having been followed through a store by security. But that day as I walked along with Rumi, we were clearly being followed. I said to him, "I think we're being followed."

He said, "Welcome to being Black in America. This is how it is for us every day."

If this goes on in New York, what's going on in the rest of the country? The problem is not over yet. This is not a Post-Racial America.

23. There but for the Grace of White Privilege Go I

So, no, I never did find Jeffrey W out there. Instead I found thousands of Jeffreys, and over two hundred of them came through my classroom. Most of them were unbelievably sweet kids. Not all the time. But, then again, who's sweet all the time?

What surprised me was how many of them were sweet most of the time. But even most of those who were thorny had something incredibly innocent about them. Many of them had done horrendous things, there's no getting around it. But are people the worst things they've ever done? Are you the worst thing you've ever done? I hope I'm not.

Given the homes that many of my students came from, I think it's amazing how well they behaved. When I look at the ratio between what many of my students were taught versus the way they behaved and I apply that ratio to my own life, I have to admit, I come up a bit short.

Sometimes it hits me that I've never been arrested. It surprises me, actually. I rebelled against my intensely religious upbringing and during my twenties and thirties I did any number of things for which I could have been arrested, and in some cases, probably should have been. But it never happened. Even when I was essentially caught, I was let go. And that, of course, is thanks to White Privilege.

One summer evening, back when possessing any quantity of marijuana was an arrestable offense, I was walking up Broadway on Manhattan's Upper West Side smoking a joint. I remember I took a good solid hit, held it in, and as I was blowing out the smoke, I looked up and saw two cops walking toward me not more than fifteen feet away.

People smoke joints differently from the way they smoke cigarettes. You don't need 20/20 vision to pick out a person who's smoking a joint even at a considerable distance. At fifteen feet, 20/100 vision would suffice. And then there's the issue of smell. Walk past a weed smoker on a hot, humid summer evening in New York City and you smell it.

I curled my fingers around the joint, not because I thought I could fool the policemen. Clearly they knew what I was up to. I did it to show I respected their authority. As they passed me, they pretended not to notice.

And just so it's clear, I did not go up to them and say, "Officers. If I were

Black, at the very least you would have spoken to me, and you may have arrested me. Therefore, I insist that you treat me that same way."

No, instead I felt lucky. And it's true. I was lucky. That kind of luck is what's known as White Privilege.

Another time after having several stiff drinks, I left a party on a holiday weekend, got in my car and came to a check point where policemen were looking for drunk drivers. The officer who spoke to me asked if I had done any drinking that evening. I said yes, I'd had a couple of drinks.

He held up his pen and told me to follow the tip of it with my eyes only, i.e., without moving my head. As he moved the pen across my field of vision, my eyes tracked the pen, but when he suddenly stopped moving it, my eyes did not stop. At that point, he should have given me a breathalyzer test. If he had, I'm quite certain I would have failed. Instead, with a look of concern, he said, "Okay, Sir. Well, drive carefully."

Please notice that I did not say, "Sir, please give me a breathalyzer test, because if I were Hispanic, I suspect you would." Instead I said, "Thank you, Officer," and I drove away very carefully, feeling lucky. And I did so without thinking about the amount of pain that made my luck possible.

And then there was the time I was exceeding the speed limit by 30 miles per hour and was stopped by a policeman. In Maine, where I was driving at the time, that is considered "criminal speeding" and is a Class E Crime. I could have lost my license for six months. I could have been fined $1,000.00. I could have been arrested and sentenced to six months in jail. None of those things happened.

And when the policeman walked up to my car, he did not have his service weapon drawn. Nor did he stand behind my window as he talked to me so that it would be difficult for me to shoot him. He did not command me to get out of the car with my hands in the air.

Instead, he walked up with a grin on his face and said, "What are you doing? The speed limit here is 45 and I don't even want to talk about how fast you were going."

I apologized—I called him "Officer"—and I explained that I'd recently bought the car and was trying it out.

He rolled his eyes. "So," he asked a little sarcastically, "are you satisfied with it?"

"Very much so, Officer," I said with a hopeful grin.

"And if I let you go with a warning, I'm not going to see you out here driving like that again. Am I?"

I did not say: "Sir, if I were an Arab, I suspect you would at the very least give me a ticket and possibly arrest me, so do your duty."

Instead, what I said was, "You will never see me speeding like that again, Officer."

Before he approached my car, he had looked up my license plate on his computer for my record. If I had been arrested for either of the previous two situations, he would have seen that, and he would have treated me in a completely different manner. Once you have one arrest under your belt, others are easier to come by. And minorities have a far easier time getting that first arrest than White people.

But I was lucky. There was nothing on my record. But as we've seen, it wasn't because I've lived such a perfect life. It was because of a special kind of luck known as White Privilege. And by the way, I don't mean to imply that those are the worst things I've ever done.

Now, you might think that the reason the policemen let me go in those three cases is the result of the friendly way I spoke to them. It's true, I was comfortable talking to them. I was comfortable because the policemen were comfortable. They were comfortable because they were White guys who were not nervous the way they might have been if I had been Black, Hispanic, or Arab.

If the officers had started yelling at me and making demands—which is the experience of many minorities in this country during encounters with policemen—I would not have been comfortable and if I had not been comfortable, I would not have responded as I did.

You'll recall that during my interview at RIEF, Ms. Cornwell had suggested that anyone's son could end up in jail. "There but for the grace of God go I," she had said. I nodded, but I did not actually agree. I knew for certain that no son of mine would ever end up in jail. Unless, of course, it was for following conscience. Otherwise, no way.

Some years after I left Rikers, one of my three sons was arrested while a college student. I won't go into details because my son asked me not to. Suffice it to say, it was for a misjudgment that hurt no one, nor was it intended to. Nor did it involve drugs or money. And let me add, that unlike myself, without anyone's encouragement, my son turned himself in after he thought about what he had done.

His lawyer encouraged both of us to write letters to the DA explaining a little bit about the situation my son had found himself in. We each spent hours writing our letters.

After reading our letters, the DA said he would drop some of the charges, but he was adamant that a couple of them would remain on his record. My son's lawyer then suggested that we write letters to the sentencing judge. We did.

It so happened that the sentencing judge was best friends with an administrator at my son's college; moreover, the judge had a couple of other things in common with my son that I won't get into. He gave my son a deferred sentence, which was a better deal than my son's lawyer had even asked for. After a year of probation and community service, the guilty plea was dropped and my son got off with a clean record.

Given that I rarely saw kids whose parents had paid their bail, most of my students on Rikers Island—Black kids, Hispanic kids, Asian kids, and White kids—came from multiple generations of disenfranchisement. Very few of them could have written confident letters to the DA and the judge, nor could their parents have done so. Most of my students didn't even know how to dress or behave in a courtroom. My son and I showed up in brand new suits and ties, clothing that revealed we respected the court, and understood the way things are done. Our clothing showed we knew the system, the game. In effect, our suits were proof of our enfranchisement.

My students had no idea about any of that. When they went to court, they dressed to impress their friends and other kids in the court room. Impressing the judge was the last thing on their minds.

If by "parent" you mean someone who is there for you, who supports you, who guides you through your first twenty years of life, an amazingly high percentage of the kids on Rikers had been orphaned at birth, just as many of their parents had been.

I suspect that this particular judge would have been fair to anyone who came before him. He struck me as a rare man capable of making shaded distinctions (I, a middle-aged White man, about whose son he judged favorably). But whether he would have been fair to my students or not, the system itself is not. It is incapable of comprehending the situation from which most of my students came.

And, by the way, my son is doing well, proving, in my mind at least, that the judge made the right call. But one reason he was able to make "the right call" is that he had things in common with my son. Each one of those points of commonality provided him with a perspective from which he could adequately view my son. "Oh, you had that experience? So did I." And, "Oh, you go to that college? I know it well. In fact, so'n'so is my best friend."

Having something in common with another person is the interpersonal equivalent of a neural pathway. It's a connection and connections are far more likely to happen when you're around your "own people." You can relate. And coincidences are far more likely to happen as well.

It is far easier to assess someone who is from your own group than it is someone from another group. You can tell by their looks who they are, and you pick up cues by the way they speak and dress. There are unconscious cues that we go by that are absent when we are dealing with people who are not part of our group. The thing is, in America, over 83% of all judges are White, while 65% of all prisoners are not White.

White Privilege and its mirror image Black Penalty (Minority Penalty) occur even when the people in power are not actively or consciously racist. Most kids who stand before a court are judged by someone who has nothing in common with them except that they are both human beings. The kids are judged according to the standards a judge would use for someone who comes from a solid family where actual values have been taught. In some cases the kids do come from good, solid families, but in many they do not. They're judged as if they come from a family with enough money to make ends meet, where the father is not absent or abusive, where the mother is not addicted to drugs. And again, sometimes that's appropriate. But regardless of the background a kid comes from, he's judged as if he comes from a good family. A family like the one the judge probably came from.

And, yes, there are judges who come from terrible circumstances and against all odds, they find their way to the top. The problem is that many of those judges have the impression that they pulled themselves up by their own bootstraps and they ignore the fact that there was someone in their lives, some adult who cared about them and gave them hope—a teacher, a coach, a clergyman, a neighbor, a doctor, a therapist. Many of the kids who stand before such judges have never had anyone like that in their lives.

According to a 2017 poll of White Americans done by NPR and the Robert Wood Johnson Foundation, a majority of American Whites believe they face discrimination.

If that's true, incarceration rates certainly don't show it: non-Hispanic Whites make up 62% of the overall US population. If White people are being treated so badly, you would think that over 62% of the US prison population would be White. In fact, only 35% of that population is White. Non-Hispanic Blacks, on the other hand, make up only 13% of the overall US population but 38% of the prison population. And it's not as if the problem is exclusively with southern states. Per capita, there are more Black prisoners than White prisoners in every state in this country.

Though non-Hispanic Whites make up 63% of the New York State population, Blacks and Hispanics make up 73% of that state's prison population. Worse yet, over a third of the state's prison population comes from five Black and Hispanic neighborhoods in New York City (the South Bronx, East New York, Harlem, Bedford-Stuyvesant, and Brownsville). There might as well be a subway line that runs from those five neighborhoods to Rikers Island and from there to the upstate prisons.

In those five neighborhoods, and many others, crime is a daily fact of life. Many of my students reported that in their neighborhoods, successful men are criminals; unsuccessful men are victims.

If I had grown up in a world like that, I wonder which way of life I would have chosen?

Epilogue

We tend to believe in progress in this country, that things are slowly getting better. And yet, during the twenty some odd years since I taught on Rikers Island, very little has changed.

Actually, I'm exaggerating. A number of things have changed. For instance, the first year I taught out there, out of every 100,000 people in the United States, 600 were in prison. By 2013, that number had risen to 900. And though it has since dropped to 698, we continue to have the world's highest rate of incarceration (ROI).

By a long shot: while the US has only 5% of the world's population, we have 25% of the world's *incarcerated* population.

According to the Prison Policy Initiative, thirty-one of our states have higher ROIs than any country in the world. That agency claims further that the state with the lowest ROI—Massachusetts—has a higher rate than all but nine countries in the world.

It's interesting to consider those nine countries: after El Salvador comes Turkmenistan, Cuba, Thailand, Rwanda, the Russian Federation, Panama, Costa Rica, and Brazil. Note how little in common the *country we claim to be* has with those nine countries, all of which are either dictatorships or have been destabilized by corruption. And though they are our primary competition in the race to lock people up, we are winning that race without breaking a sweat.

Other industrialized democracies have rates that are far lower than ours: for instance, France, Canada, and England/Wales lock up fewer than 150 of their citizens per 100,000. Norway, Germany, and Italy lock up fewer than 100, while the numbers for Sweden, Finland, Denmark, and the Netherlands are below 60. And then there is Japan that locks up just 45 of its people for every 100,000—that's 6.4% of our 698.

We call ourselves the "Land of the Free," but we are also the land that deprives more people of their freedom than any other. And most of those people are minorities.

In the midst of all of this, there is some potentially good news: I applaud Bill de Blasio, mayor of New York City, for taking steps to close Rikers Island within the next decade. The bad news is new jails will be built to replace the island. To believe that new jails alone will solve the problems that have plagued Rikers Island is highly optimistic. Nothing will change unless large numbers of personnel are replaced by people who actually care. This would include many police officers and COs (and many of their bosses), many prosecutors, and many judges. In addition, court-appointed lawyers need to be paid something that approaches the salaries of other lawyers. In fact, if all of those changes were made, closing Rikers would not appear as urgent.

Notes

[1] The difference in the sentences meted out to Blacks and Whites says it all: according to the US Sentencing Commission, on average, Black men receive sentences that are 19% longer than those of White men. And by the way, that's for the same exact crimes. And that's after considering such variables as criminal history, age, and education.

People sometimes dismiss those sorts of statistics with the claim that White people don't commit crime at the same rate as Blacks and Hispanics. Let's make believe that's true. What reason do White people have to commit crime? Most of us can get what we want without stealing. For many minorities in this country, that is not the case.

There are Whites who say, "Yeah, we can get what we want without stealing—it's called getting a job." The thing is, for many minorities, getting a job is nearly impossible.

[2] That building is now called the Robert N. Davoren Center (RNDC).

[3] I never heard an explanation concerning why only men taught in the Sprungs. I suspect it had something to do with safety. Getting there was impossible without walking down incredibly long corridors, and more than half of those walks required one to pass a file of twenty or more adult male inmates who were being led by a single CO. At times it felt dangerous.

[4] While that is what I believed about the word "fuck" at the time, I have since learned there is no proof that the word was in use as early as 1066.

[5] Using the word "staying" rather than "living" always haunted me. The fact is, many of my students on Rikers did not live in a place. They stayed there, as in, "we stayed in a motel." The word choice said it all. Nothing felt permanent in their worlds. Many of them had moved dozens of times since they were children. As a result, their lives had the feel of something temporary. And granted life is temporary. But children from stable homes are shielded from that for far longer than most of these kids were.

[6] A few weeks after that, I sat in on one of Dr. Steele's classes during my prep period. The kids had so much respect for this man I was blown away. It didn't take long for me to understand why: a student asked him where in Africa the slaves had come from. From memory, Dr. Steele drew a map on the board of the continent that included the borders of all 54 countries.

He shaded in and named the countries from where most of the slaves had come, and with arrows labeled the percentage each of those countries had contributed. That was just one of the many times I observed his prodigious memory.

[7] I don't know what "Bing" stood for—was it an acronym? Whatever it was, the Bing was a place they put kids as a way of punishing them, a jail within a jail, the juvenile equivalent of solitary confinement. In January of 2015, Rikers Island stopped solitary confinement for inmates under the age of 21.

[8] And yes, at that time, kids could still buy cigarettes at the commissary even though the minimum age for buying cigarettes was 18 and many of our students were 16. That has since changed.

[9] "Burner" did not yet apply to a phone.

[10] I can only recall the face and name of one of the White kids I had. White Tony was Italian American from one of the outer boroughs. When he first arrived, he didn't say much. He was sitting near the perimeter of the class, though I was pretty sure he liked me. You could usually tell who had the power in a class by where they sat. It was kind of like chess: kids who occupied the center had the most power. Unless, that is, they didn't like you. If a kid didn't like a particular teacher, he might elect to sit on the perimeter of the classroom to make a kind of statement. Kids who had status and who liked a teacher, sat in the middle of the classroom. Of course there were exceptions, but not often.

At any rate, within a couple days, White Tony was sitting in the center of the classroom and he was talking like the Black kids. It was fairly obvious that he had acquired some status. He'd use the word "nigga" the way the Black kids used it. He'd say things like, "Yo, nigga, that's what I be tellin' you." None of the Black kids batted an eye when he spoke this way. He was the only White kid I saw out there who used that word without a trace of self-consciousness or fear. I saw other kids try, but there was something different about the way White Tony did it. Within two weeks he was out on bail.

[11] I was sad to learn that Mr. Mitchell, Mr. Cumberbatch, and Mr. Rhodes have all died during the past several years.

[12] I took public transportation a couple of times when my car wouldn't start. It took me just about exactly an hour and a half to travel six point three miles. Even in New York traffic, I could drive there in less than twenty minutes.

[13] I actually don't remember if the term the kids used for masturbating was

"catchin' money" or "makin' money." A friend who taught on the island claims it was "catchin' money," but I remember it as "makin' money." On the other hand, I agree that "Money" was a nickname used for any young kid, as in "Yo, Money…" so "catchin' money" made sense.

[14] Some of that advantage comes from the trillions of today's dollars that were added by slave labor to the wealth of this entire country. And though thousands of White families (both in the South and the North) benefited directly from this, as did hundreds of corporations (both in the South and in the North), every White family that's been in this country for two centuries or more benefited indirectly during the slavery years when the cost of goods would have been more expensive had it not been for free labor. I wonder how many of the currently wealthy White American families would have been less wealthy (or perhaps not even wealthy at all) if slaves had actually been paid for their labor.

Jason Trask taught English to young incarcerated men at the Rikers Island Educational Facility from 1991 - 1994. Later, he moved to Maine where he established and taught in an off-site alternative education program for high school students who hate school. He now writes in the Western Foothills of Maine where he lives with his wife. He has three adult sons. His novel *I'm Not Muhammad* was published in 2011.